CW00825692

SCIENTISM
EXPOSED

Hiding the True Creator of Creation

Robbie Davidson

Acknowledgments

First and foremost, I thank Jesus for creating me and giving me an opportunity to expose the world's lies with my documentary films and now with my first book. I owe Him my all in everything that I do and it's only Him that I wish to glorify with the work He has set out for me to do.

I have come to understand that one of the greatest privileges anyone can enjoy in life is to be blessed with and surrounded by people who appreciate you and love you unconditionally and stand by you in your destiny assignment. I am blessed to have many such people in my life. I would like to appreciate my dear wife, Rachel Davidson who stood by me when it came to the point that I had to obey the call of God on my life. I love you sweetie. I appreciate you more than words can say. My Children: Kiara, Sophia and Robbie Jr. I'm so blessed with such an amazing family and my prayer is that I can be the husband and father that God wants me to be for you all. I thank my parents Bryan and Mary for all their love and support with everything I truly believed in and wanted to accomplish in life. Thank you to Pastor Jerry Jackson & his entire family from True Life Baptist Church for all your support and welcoming me and my family the way you have. Thanks to the many that are on the frontlines with me in this battle, exposing some of the biggest lies, with this war on truth.

I thank everyone that has encouraged me, supported me and walked with me through one of the most eye-opening revelations in my journey so far.

Blessings,

-Robbie Davidson

Preface

We live in a world where the idea of 'truth' has been altered and transformed in ways the human brain can barely comprehend anymore. Our values, our thoughts, and our perception are molded in such a manner to benefit those powerful few who hide behind the curtain, the puppeteers who push us and laugh at our disorientation.

Their methods are vicious, always aiming at confusing us, because through confusion, they can rise above and rule the rest of us like flocks of sheep. Throughout the ages, various methods were used to brainwash and force the masses into submission, ranging from brute force to the propagation of brilliant lies.

Right now, the world is confronted with an illogical phenomenon, Scientism, a deadly religion that must be neither debated nor questioned. The scientist comes forth like a saint and we must embrace his theories as pure truth, regardless of the facts or hidden intentions.

We're told that we need to believe, we need to not question or wonder about the validity of the so called 'scientific truths'. This isn't science anymore; this is more like a collective madness, where people are pushed aside and considered nothing but freaks of nature... An accident that might as well have never happened.

Over the years, the science proved its utility to mankind; the true, fact-based science cured illnesses and helped us live a better life, but at the same time, a different branch evolved. Drugged by their importance and the attention they received, the members of this current system of thought replaced God with their own persona, they glorified their name and their agenda, while we just stood in the shadows and watched the spectacle.

This new religion begins to call us heretics if we dare to oppose its theories, and soon, we'll go back to the dark ages, where we will not possess the courage to open our mouths and speak the truth, even if it's right in front of our eyes. If analyzed in more detail, we can observe the war between the old and the new. The old being our long-lasting religions and the idea of divinity and the new being the new religion and its intrusive ways.

We see all over the media how science is glorified, while religion is cast aside. We are encouraged from the earliest years of life through school, to see Scientism as the only way. Its aggressiveness is dubious, and one might think there must be a hidden agenda somewhere, that someone or some group is trying to blind us to the truth.

The light is all around us and yet, we fail to see it as we are pushed to focus on a single, dark dot. We're nothing in this universe, a speck of dust, appearing here by chance; a speck of dust that will fade away as quickly as it came into being, and in the end, we will be completely forgotten.

It's time to pull back the veil of Scientism, exposing many of the greatest deceptions in the world to hide the true Creator of creation.

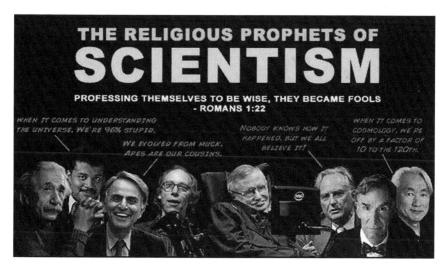

Table of contents:

Chapter 1: An Introduction to Scientism

"O Timothy, keep that which is committed to thy trust, avoiding profane and vain babblings, and oppositions of science falsely so called:" 1Timothy 6:20

While Scientism has been active on earth for millennia, many have never heard the word before. To provide an appropriate backdrop for my extensive inquiry into this thing called Scientism, it is pertinent to define Scientism as clearly as possible.

It is also important to quickly define Science here for purposes of clarity. Science is simply a method of inquiry and also refers to the knowledge gained from this inquiry. The scientific method, which might be familiar to many, consists of such steps as observation, hypothesizing, experimenting, and theorizing.

It may be very surprising for many to hear, but no theory proposed in the world of science is considered final. The original tenets of science depend on the belief that all theories are subject to scrutiny and re-examination. It is assumed that every theory, no matter how brilliant it sounds, will be proven false and replaced, if only by a more comprehensive theory.

This nature of science shows that at its heart, it is a very open process, which admits its fallibility and uncertainty, while remaining on the quest for truth.

Scientism is the belief that the methods of science are superior to any other method of determining truth. While science believes a thing because it has been observed or "proven" to be true, Scientism, on the other hand, believes a thing because science says it is true.

Scientism, therefore, is a school of thought that blindly accords science a heavy superiority without acknowledging the loopholes or non-absoluteness of findings, as done by science itself.

Because of this attribute of Scientism, clearly it can be a dangerous thought process. Scientism is not the same thing as "Science," rather, it is a faulty epistemology or theory of knowledge that has its origins in the massive success of the process called Science. Scientism is, in fact, a religion dressed up as something else.

In the world we live in today, Scientism comes easily, almost naturally, to many of us. If a concept or idea has been proven by science, we immediately take it to be true, even when we neither conducted the experiments ourselves nor analyzed the data obtained from these experiments. In our minds, because science says something has been discovered, it must be true.

The Force behind Scientism (and Its Agenda)

Scientism, with all its masquerading as a champion of truth and knowledge, is not so benign. What lies beneath the shiny veneer of research and experiments is the existence of a clear anti-God agenda. This agenda is clear enough to be seen by anybody who looks close enough.

It has become clear to me that there is a lot of stuff masquerading as science and there's a force behind that. This can only be a manifestation of man's perpetual adversary; whose primary mission is to tell lies about everything and keep people from the truth of God.

This adversary, the Deceiver, is more powerful than we think, mostly because we have come to underestimate what we were warned about clearly in Scripture.

The signs are clearly visible, but we might need to dig deeper into the Bible, because we have become far removed from the original languages the Great Book was originally written in. Therefore, it is important that believers everywhere study what the Bible has to say about creation, sin, and salvation.

Scientism does not exist merely for its own sake, but neither does it exist for the propagation of truth and enlightenment. If that were the case, then strict science would be enough. While science is as secular as can be, Scientism is spiritual. Over the years, it has become clear to me that Scientism is a spiritual deception and a spiritual agenda masquerading as fact, when the theories put forth are only theories of men coming from evil origins to discredit the truth of God's Word.

Part of the great danger inherent to Scientism is its ability to rope people in using thought processes and patterns, which it falsely refers to as logic. Most of these processes are only traps based on theories, theories which are mere speculation and not as concrete as everybody thinks they are.

I think that everyone of us has wondered, at some point, at the outlandish claims made by science. Somehow, we still give science a pass and continue to believe in it blindly.

For example, evolution cannot be proven through the scientific method, but hardly any report on this has been featured by any major news outlet or establishment, which is a clear indicator that they are not interested in giving people the science of an issue but the Scientism of it.

Staunch believers of the Word of God do not discredit science. In fact, they see science as a great thing, if its limitations are acknowledged. They also worry about the spiritual nature of Scientism, since it is a belief system, a religion, and one which has set out to destroy the credibility of the Word of God. Destruction of this credibility leads to the destruction of the credibility of God in people's minds and makes them doubt the existence of a creator.

This sinister agenda is not a new endeavor. Attempts at discrediting God have been in effect from the early moments of history, as far back as the events of Genesis, Chapter 3, when the Deceiver, Satan, tried to plant doubts in the mind of Adam and Eve, and, unfortunately, he succeeded.

These attempts have not stopped and, in some ways, the Deceiver is still succeeding today. This is evident in all the times people read the Scriptures and end up asking questions like, "Did God really mean that?" or "Did God mean that literally?"

All these situations of doubt arise mostly because believers play loosely with the Word of God. Opponents of Scientism are quick to state that the Bible is neither a science book nor a history book, but every time it discusses matters of science or history, it turns out to be accurate. Could this be a mere coincidence? I think not!

I find it utterly saddening that the Bible is being reduced to "just a book" or a "work of literature," when, in fact, it is more than that. It's the actual Word of God and we should take Him at His Word.

You should all open your eyes to the truth, but over the decades and centuries, we have been led down strange paths. Our minds and perceptions have been twisted and turned through 'education' and restless propaganda, thus we need to recover from our deep slumber and face the truth again.

Just think about the way in which an impostor rejoices in the laurels of the true inventor, stealing his or her glory and adoration, and, in the process, turning it into something toxic. The choice turns into submission and, slowly but surely, we are denied the chance to wonder about the truth.

I think it is time for us to take a break and analyze the two phenomena, because there is a clear distinction between science and Scientism. Yes, they are completely opposite, even if the syllables are almost the same.

Science is a method of inquiry, where the knowledge acquired by that method is tested again and again, until there is no shred of doubt regarding the results. The scientific method follows a clear path: it all starts with a hypothesis, is then followed by experiments, careful observation, and, in the end, the scientist draws the logical conclusions.

Another aspect that is definitive for true science is the fact that no theory is considered final, and there is always a place for contradictions and improvements. Over the years, it has been proven how older theories have been replaced by new ones, as science and technology evolved along with mankind. With every passing year, we grow smarter as a species, and this does not come from accepting 'universal truths' proposed by dubious individuals, but rather from questioning everything and looking for better answers.

Possibilities will always be endless if all theories are subjected to scrutiny and reexamination, and I say this because, in a world of billions, no individual or small group of individuals can say they hold the definitive truth.

On the other hand, Scientism fails to look at the essential part of the scientific process, and I would say that it does so on purpose. This belief that the methods of science are superior to any other ways of determining truth is flawed and damaging.

Science believes things because they have been observed and tested to be true, while Scientism believes things because science says they are true. This is nothing but a toxic paradox of the human existence.

Just close your eyes for a moment and imagine how a stranger comes to you and tells you that your parents are not actually your parents and that you must believe this as the ultimate truth, with no option of searching for the truth on your own. Maybe, with this example in mind, you will grasp the level of absurdity Scientism proposes for us.

Unfortunately, most of us accept it, because we've been indoctrinated since we first opened our eyes. The school, the media, and almost every other aspect of our lives have been flooded with false theories and truths, which we had to accept, unless we wanted to become pariahs.

This is a harsh truth, but I feel forced to say it, because this is the only path that could lead to our awakening. Most of us are guilty of Scientism, to some extent, but it does not mean that it is our fault. We have been raised in a system where Science stood above God, and where the scientists and their words were even more important than scripture. Our society has been brainwashed into thinking that scientists can never be wrong and that everything they say is true, although most of their hypotheses are actually nothing but hypotheses, never tested or proved in any way.

Even if tests have been conducted, we weren't there to check the results, thus we have no guarantee, and our only option is to take their word for it.

If you ask me, I think it's strange how we have all been pushed to a place where we take everything for granted, including the scientists' words. We never question anything and live our lives based mostly on how others tell us to live it. Somehow, they made us stupid, and I say this with all my heart, because we look at those men and women dressed in white coats and say to ourselves, "they should know better, they are smarter than me, they're scientists!"

I am sure most of us did this at least once in our lifetime, and this is wrong! We are all capable of thinking for ourselves. We are capable enough to look for the truth and find what really matters to us. We do not need anyone to dictate to us when or what we should think or believe.

Life isn't really that complicated if you decide to open your eyes and see for yourself, but that's the problem, isn't it? Scientism tends to distort everything and make it look complicated, so we just jump into our dark corner and wait for them to explain things for us, just like little children in kindergarten.

Listen to me when I tell you that truth is always simple. Truth always stands where little assumption can be found. That is why elaborate lies have been concocted, so that we do not understand anything anymore, and thus we can stay docile and nod our heads in approval, whenever they throw something at us.

This tendency to quickly believe in the absolute nature of science can be explained by a principle called Occam's razor. Occam's razor is a problem-solving principle that, in its simplest form, states that whenever two theories exist that explain the same observation, the one that requires the least number of assumptions is true.

To Apply Occam's Razor:

1. Determine how many assumptions and conditions are necessary for each explanation to be correct.

2. If an explanation requires extra assumptions or conditions, demand evidence commensurate with the strength of each claim.

3. Extraordinary claims require extraordinary evidence.

Strangely, Occam's razor points to Scripture as absolute truth, when addressing matters where it takes a stand that differs from that of Scientism. When there is a literal interpretation of the Scriptures and it defines certain concepts properly, there is absolutely no need to heed the opinions of science, which work on many different assumptions. Consequently, when Scripture and science clash, as they do very frequently, the shortest road to truth is believing Scripture and investigating the claims made by mainstream science. Also, remember, when it comes to biblical interpretation, if the plain sense makes sense, then seek no other sense.

For almost two millennia, humanity grew and developed along the Word of God, we knew and understood its meaning, because we knew the Word of God was truth, and that truth was all we needed. But as we started to come out of the Middle Ages, a battle was waged, where certain people began to doubt the Word of God, thinking that Scientism was above it. The Bible was cast aside, denounced to be telling only fables and mythology.

The war between the fathers of the church and the leaders of the enlightenment was on, and God was put in the balance with science. Their philosophers kept saying that God is dead, and a new age was ready to emerge, one where doubt and speculation had no place, and only strong facts and testing can determine the truth.

This was a frontal attack, with all the 'weapons' in their arsenal being thrown at once, because the 'enlightened ones' hoped they would have their victory, the first and final one.

Old theories and ideas were taken down, replaced by the new science, so fast and so decisive that, for a while, people could not tell what was truth or fiction anymore. Indeed, both sides tried to hold their ground, but, in the end, it looked like the science was settled and the Bible had finally lost the battle to the means of discovering truth.

The paradigm had changed, and people's minds had changed with it. There was, indeed, an underground struggle that never actually faded away, but religion never got the power to fight back at full might. Science was queen and she looked like she was going to reign over mankind for eternity.

For some reason, science and scripture are placed on the same level. They can only be enemies and can't work in symbiosis for the betterment of humanity. This idea has been propagated throughout society, convincing people that they had to choose between God and Science.

I have no idea why I cannot believe in God and Science at the same time, and now, we see how 'all scientists' declared that God and Science are irreconcilable. Now, more than ever, we look in the mirror and see ourselves as gods. The scientists keep bragging that they will unlock the power of God, eventually. Yet, I look at things differently, and analyze them in depth. We might have cracked the power of the atom and created some of the most destructive weapons the world has ever seen, and countless other things created with technology, but we will never reach the might of God.

This puny arrogance we throw around will certainly backfire, because we can never compare ourselves to God, regardless of how much technological advancement we achieve.

We reached this point, mainly, because science is no longer science anymore. Where true science is the scientific method or empirical data. What started as science back then, has evolved into something that we cannot recognize anymore, we can't understand it, or break it into small bits, and all we are pushed to do is to believe in it!

What if this is the new religion of the world? A religion with hidden means and purposes, that's not calling itself as a religion, a trick of the mind, a lie that blames the true religion for being a lie?

I call this "a nasty paradox", because that is exactly what it is! A phenomenon where all its members are blaming God and the scriptures for deceiving people, but, at the same time, they try so desperately to take its place, posing as something else, while, all the way, they crave the same adulation. Scientism must be loved and adored unconditionally, just because some people say so. Well, if you ask me, this is pure lunacy.

This new world religion, which spreads its tentacles over people's minds, both on display and in covertness, is full of fabrication and has an anti-God agenda. For them, the end results excuse the means through which they reach those goals and no sacrifice is too much, regardless of whether this means that they are brainwashing millions of people and making them lose their sense of life, in the end.

The Bible says that God created the Earth and the universe in six days and rested on the seventh day, while Scientism states that our earth is billions of years old, with ages upon ages, extinct species, and so on. They mock the Bible and God's Word, while ridiculing the fact that certain people say the Earth is only six to ten thousand years old, believe in a worldwide flood, or accept that we were all created from Adam and Eve, which goes against the evolutionary narrative. How else does Scientism respond to these type of people? They have gone so far as to say that it's child abuse if anyone dares to teach their children the literal truth of the Bible when it comes to creation!

Ridicule is their primary weapon, a weapon they have built over time, and now, they use it with the utmost viciousness, attacking everything and everyone, who dares to oppose their theories. That's all they have, no facts, no proofs, or anything of that sort, and they attack continuously, so they can stay in power. They're using the same old principle, divide and conquer, and now, they've added ridicule to the process.

The Bible tells us how we're special in this universe, how we have a meaning and a certain place to fill that was designed especially for us, but when they came along, they threw all that away, stripping us naked of our uniqueness. To Scientism, we're nothing but a freak occurrence of nature, a random accident that could have easily never happened, a speck of dust at the edge of the galaxy and the universe itself, something that does not really matter in the greater game of life.

At first, we rebelled against this idea, because we had been taught over the years that God loves us and that He sent us into this world to serve a precise purpose that only we could accomplish. With time, they pushed this idea into our heads and somehow managed to convince us that they're right. We stopped thinking about it and took their theories as the inarguable truth, because they're scientists and they must know more than we do.

The end game of their vicious struggle is to exclude God from society completely, and from people's hearts, as well. The process

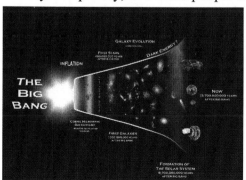

started decades ago, if not hundreds of years ago, and it has been successful, to a certain extent. Just look around you and see how many atheists there are and how many individuals who repudiate God, thinking the universe just popped out of nowhere, coming from nothing, suddenly. The problem remains for the Agnostic, Atheist and Anti-theist—if there never was a Creator there could not have been any creating, yet we have a verifiable creation. To put it simply, 0 x 0 can never = 1. Those who posit a Creatorless universe cannot explain how matter and energy just happened to exist [acknowledging that these are fundamentally two forms of the same phenomenon]. Matter and energy lack the ability to create themselves. Something with a conscious will and amazing power had to precede them in reality, and create the most fundamental building blocks of existence.

Those who at present do not believe must conclude that random coincidence caused random events through infinitely long periods of time to enable random mutations which caused the first cell which through statistically inconceivable amounts of time led to humankind. They assert this even though it violates the Second Law of Thermodynamics or entropy. As a result of this refusal to accept Causation, they therefore assume humanity has no purpose, life is meaningless, there is no hope for eternity; so live only for today.

Right now, there is a battle going on in people's minds, the young generations, who represent the future. The Scientism members have been and are still waging war against people's mindsets and moral principles, because they know that the best and easiest way to control people is to teach them what to think and how to think. For Scientism, the greatest danger is represented by an individual who uses his mind to judge and analyze, to wonder and seek the truth. For that reason, they are investing immense efforts and resources to control education, thus the way children think. By changing the paradigm, they know they will be able to change and control the world in their favor.

The one who is propagating this agenda and working through the Scientism apostates, as I often like to call them, is clever. He knows the human psyche and how people's minds work, thus, he knows where to strike for maximum effect. A weak, untrained mind is no match for him. Satan knows that most of us are short-sighted and look around in order to guide our lives, when we are not firmly anchored in the Word of God as our final authority in all matters.

We're social creatures and we often compare ourselves to those surrounding us, friends, relatives, colleagues. We want to be like our siblings, because this helps us fit in better, but this is also our greatest weakness. The members of the Scientism community realized that our fear of being rejected can sometimes be stronger than our fear of God, thus we would adopt any idea to be accepted and embraced.

For this feeling of belonging, we're willing to accept things we don't always believe in, but we still do it. They knew that they had to convince a sufficient number of people, and then, the process would become automatic. Parents would teach their children the new doctrine and so on, and every time some individual dared to oppose their teachings, they subjected that individual to public scrutiny.

They will mock you for standing your ground, regardless of whether you have all the facts and proofs. They will laugh at you and try to make you feel small and unimportant, and if the safety will stay in numbers, they'll cover your voice with background noise.

Moreover, if you play in the same arena, they have another weapon to use against you. Countless scientists, who tested and proved Scientism theories to be flawed, were and still are forced to keep their mouths shut, unless they want to lose their jobs, their prestige, and their livelihoods. Scientism will stop at nothing to achieve its goals, regardless of how many proofs you have. If you are against their flawed doctrine, then you have no chance!

The master puppeteers control the scientific publications, including all the means for one to publish and show to the world their breakthroughs. They censor, they scrutinize, and they bury everything that stands against them, and I guess this might be one of the reasons why they compare themselves to God so much. With so much power to control the world, they must feel that they can never be wrong, thus, the indoctrination of the masses is the next logical step for them.

I say it is time for us to snap out of this trance and jump out of the mousetrap. Stop running in vain and look around, ask yourself if this is what you believe, what you want. It only takes a moment.

Stop looking at this Trojan Horse called Scientism, as if it is supposed to be some sort of wonder that is going to change our lives, because it will certainly change things, but only for the worse.

Scientism is not trying to be a mere world religion, but a dictatorship of the mind, too. And if, at first, it started mildly with trying to convince people, with time, it will uncover its true nature, a beast set on destroying everything in its path.

Their propaganda is strong, continuous, and only focuses on the emotions of the people. There's nothing backing it, no facts, no truth, but merely a continuous stream of allegations and false ideas, thrown out as loudly as possible. They probably think that one who is the loudest will always hold the truth, but this idea can only work in pairage with ignorance.

When people are ignorant and too lazy to look for the truth themselves, this technique will have an effect, but otherwise, it's useless and futile. I know for a fact that an educated person will always be able to differentiate between true science and Scientism, as Scientism is nothing but religious beliefs clothed in scientific terms. A lie will always be a lie, regardless of how well it tries to disguise itself as truth. The evidence will always be there for all those who decide to look objectively. When analyzing a situation, you need to keep your mind clear of any misconceptions that Scientism throws at you. Otherwise, if you accept to look through the lens of the world, your perception will be altered, and you will stray far from the truth.

Right now, we live in a world where nothing is what it appears to be, a world of deception and fogging mirrors. I feel like God's warning of the Deceiver has finally come to age, and there are powerful forces pushing this 'non-science'. This hidden spiritual agenda is trying to win over our souls and minds by all means necessary, and by infiltrating and corrupting our morals and beliefs, they hope to change our reality.

The dark forces behind Scientism are parading ideas and theories that have nothing to do with God. In fact, they contradict and try to replace God in all aspects of our lives.

This wolf dressed in sheepskin keeps bashing the Bible, trying to disprove God's Word, but at a closer look, we realize how the Bible is completely accurate about all the aspects it approaches, be it science, history, etc. The Bible is not a science or history book, nor simply a book of literature, as they call it, but it is the Word of God, and every single word in the Bible bears more meaning than all the books in this world put together.

Truth has always been important to me – as it probably is to many of us – but I've always pushed myself further, always gone out of my way to find it. While in this state of mind, at some point in my life, I realized something: numerous ideas explaining the state of our world floated around as fact, and as "logical" as they sounded, these explanations were unproven.

I could have let them go, of course, but I couldn't. As a Christian, it rang constantly in my head that I had a responsibility to uphold the truth and point out deception, wherever I encountered it. To do this, I was willing to read, research, and find out the truth, and then, share my findings with the rest of the world.

What I found out was mind-blowing. For centuries, we have been fed a huge lie, disguised as science. While science can be considered true on its own terms, and up to the point where its limits begin, what we've been fed is Scientism, a falsehood disguised as scientific truth.

In fact, if we took the time to follow scientific procedure, we would see that it's nowhere near as infallible as many proponents of

Scientism have tried to make us believe and have mostly succeeded in doing so. True science, when conducted and followed properly, turns out to be a humbling experience, a learning adventure that shows us that there is always something beyond the reach of our senses.

True science is a reminder of our humanity and the need for a relationship with our Creator. It is also a reminder that the truth is a value higher than us. Acknowledging this fact of our systematic deceit over the years leaves us with two questions:

- What is the truth they've been hiding?

- Are we willing to go as far as possible and necessary to get this truth?

I was, still am, and so should you be.

Chapter 2: Scientism and Evolution

"In the beginning, God created the heavens and the earth. And the earth was without form, and void; and darkness was upon the face of the deep. And the Spirit of God moved upon the face of the waters."
Suddenly, God spoke into the darkness…
And God said, "Let there be light."

As you all should know, this is the beginning of Genesis in the Bible, where it is told how God created everything in six days. God spoke everything into existence. There was no evolution, no billions of years where species popped up and faded away, and no primordial soup where cells appeared out of nothing when a lucky lightning bolt struck.

The theories of Scientism exclude God from the creation process completely and they replace him with… nothing. If I were to believe these people, then everything came into being just like that, for no apparent reason, and it all happened at a random time, because, why not?

The Scientism agenda leans so heavily on the theory of evolution that, without it, it would fall apart within seconds. Evolution itself is strongly intertwined with the Big Bang theory, the idea that an explosion of energy (from supposedly nothing) gave birth to the first life form, which, over the years, has underwent many stages and become the many species we see on earth today.

Evolution, as famously put forward by Charles Darwin, is so ubiquitous in our schools and other institutions that very few question its validity.

The central argument of evolution for the case of Scientism is that if humans have evolved to what we are today from an accidental, purposeless process, then, clearly, there is no way we could have been created by a God, and consequently, there is no need to believe in him.

Furthermore, any moral truths handed down by this God stand nullified and, therefore, we have no obligation to live our lives by this moral code. Considering how Scientism touts science as "empirical truth," it is easy to see how many people have come to view everything else as purely subjective, including concepts such as good, evil, love, beauty, malice, happiness, grief, and ethics.

This particularly stiff-necked view of life tells us that the physical world is all that exists. Sadly, many have come to acknowledge this as truth, even in the face of phenomena like dreams, extrasensory perception, and miracles; phenomena which science has no clear explanation for, and which scientism has therefore denounced as untrue.

It is this idea, that we all evolved from some random speck of cell billions of years ago, that allows radical scientists to justify their use of human beings as mere objects, which they can inspect and experiment on freely. Of course, the point of using a human as a lab rat reduces him to the position occupied by the lab rat – an object to be controlled and manipulated.

Evolution is surely a hard sell for an individual who hasn't been badgered with the theory all their life. This is why, from the earliest age possible, the backers of Scientism have made it compulsory that children hear this theory and internalize it as the plain truth.

The truth is, Scientism has its roots in the Big Bang theory and evolutionism. It can't work without these two, but it can't explain them either, so it all rests on a theoretical level. Untested theories we need to take for granted, because they think that we have no alternative, but they're wrong, and I am going to explain this further.

Now, think about it, if we were created through a material, purposeless process, where everything happens randomly, with cells mutating without a specific set of rules or higher purpose, then there's no need for you to believe in a God. After all, this decaying flesh is all there is, and once you die, you rot and disappear from history forever. This way of thinking is flawed and wicked. Unfortunately, by using this fake science, Satan has managed to lower the credibility of the Bible over the years, convincing more and more people to turn their backs on God.

Their success rested on the ignorance of people and on the fact that science is an objective knowledge, while religion is perceived as a subjective need. As a result, Scientism demanded that religion needs to subordinate its claims about the world to those of science or fall into the shadows.

If you claim that you don't believe in evolution, they'll call you names, such as ignorant, stupid, or completely insane. It is a risk most people don't have the courage to take. That happens for a good reason, because, as I have stated previously, we all want to be accepted, we want to be a part of something bigger than ourselves.

When Darwin came up with the idea of the evolution of species, including the evolution of man, people were rather skeptical about this new theory. Darwin himself had his own setbacks in convincing people that everything evolved from a cell and then turned into the most intelligent being the earth has ever seen, and yet, in the end, the Theory of Evolution was here to stay.

Although it was just a theory, standing on Darwin's speculations, it was imposed as mainstream eventually, and soon, teachers started teaching Darwin's outlandish ideas to children in schools.

This was not the first attempt to replace God's Word though, as throughout the centuries, people have tried relentlessly to distort and transform God's Word to suit their purposes. With Darwin and his theories of evolution, the dark forces had, in their hands, the perfect tool to finally complete their mission.

Scientism underlines the fact that science is the controlling mechanism of all life and at first, science was, indeed, responsible for studying nature and its intriguing mechanisms. Unfortunately for science and its limited means, it could not go beyond the mechanical aspects of nature and could not comprehend nor analyze things such as love, compassion, ethics, beauty, good, evil, and consciousness. Science did not possess the necessary tools to analyze and classify these aspects of nature and human life, thus, in the end, it tried to morph them into something less extraordinary.

By doing this, Scientism has reduced humans to mere objects that can be inspected, experimented on, and, ultimately, controlled. By turning man from a divine creature into an accident of nature, Scientism somehow managed to push aside all the divine attributes, such as the soul and human consciousness, and made us look like pigs that are ready to go to slaughter and have nothing to say about it.

I feel really sad to see what has become of us; how man has turned against man in a battle that makes no sense, which began because some of us started believing they are better than the rest and therefore, have the right to truth and rule.

In 1922, J. K. Chesterton warned that Scientism has become a creed, taking over our institutions, a system of thought, which began with evolution and has ended in eugenics. I believe, though, that it began much earlier, with the heliocentric universe, the story of our solar system, and the Big Bang theory, which created the perfect premise for the introduction of biological evolution later on.

If we are to investigate Scientism on a deeper level, I say we should start with the theory of evolution and its fabricated millions and billions of years of primordial history and the countless eras it proposes.

It would appear that the entire scientific community embraced and backed Darwin's theory of evolution as the only truth regarding the origins of life on earth, but, in fact, this whole spectacle, with colorful drawings in textbooks, is nothing but a grand charade, an elaborate lie that managed to fool millions of people. These are the only true millions in this story, the millions of people who were tricked into believing something that never really existed.

The Bible tells us to raise our heads and look up at the sky if we really want to witness the might of God. It is right there, right under our noses, we must simply look at the heavens to realize the truth, to see the intelligent design of our world. Scientism claims that everything happened to be the way it is by chance, but I smell the lie that's being thrown at me. I can't believe that everything in this world fits so perfectly, and that it all happened hazardously, that God had nothing to do with it, because God does not exist.

Randomness brings chaos, not beauty and order. If you don't believe me, just leave your garden unattended, and you'll see what happens. The weeds will grow wildly and your flowers will disappear… that's not what happened with the Earth. Here, everything is in balance, nature, the weather, the oceans, and everything else; they all work in perfect harmony.

The real battle is in our minds, and Satan, who is the father of lies, knows the best tools and when to use them. The Devil is not going to show up at your door, one late evening, and force you to sign a deal with him; he is much cleverer than that. That's not how he can win you over, but if he can get you to think in the wrong way, if he can make you think exactly what he wants you to think, then the battle is over.

And Satan does not come to you directly, because he uses the same ways as God, and that's by working through people. People who, for some reason, have chosen the path of the darkness and are now trying to lead everyone else onto that path, and Scientism is currently the best way to do so.

Your mind is your most precious asset and that's because it is free from all external influence. Neither God nor the Devil can grab it directly and make it think one way or another. God strictly forbade this from happening, so, all that's left is for the Devil to conquer it indirectly, through manipulation and propaganda. The end goal is to make you think that you want something or believe in something, when, in fact, you've been the subject of manipulation and trickery.

If we analyze evolution even more, we can see that Scientism proposes two main ideas:

Idea number one: all living beings on this earth share a common ancestor. I mentioned them before, and this means we are related, to some extent, with all living beings. So, I am related to a chimp, which some might say has certain similarities, like two legs and two arms. At the same time, I am related to a fungus too... Isn't that crazy? I could look at a fungus for a month and I still would not see any similarities between that thing and me. Anyway, I am sure those 'scientists' will see similarities even in a rock.

Idea number two: the force that pushed the evolutionary process onward was a blind, undirected process of natural selection, where every mutation happened randomly in nature.

In Darwin's view, the evolution of species was an unguided, blind purposeless process that simply happened. Why did it happen? Well, don't ask me, I do not hold the answers to such preposterous concepts.

Now, let me tell you something else. Science as a discipline managed to prove certain aspects of our life, through testing and experimenting. But at the same time, while resting on the laurels of the past, they applied the same principles to concepts that can't actually be tested and observed.

Things such as the origin of life and the universe can never be observed, and yet, the scientists assumed that if they were right about some aspects, then they must be right about others too. It's wrong, it's flawed, and the worst part of it all is the fact that they are trying to convince the rest of us, one way or another, to adopt their worldviews, or religion, which is what I like to call it.

This made up theology we call Scientism needs those gaps and those millions and billions of years, because it is incapable of properly explaining its theories, thus, it throws all sorts of unbelievable outlandish ideas at us and asks us to take them as truths. They find a bone and recreate the whole animal from it, without having any idea of what that animal looked like. Somehow, they think they acquired the authority to play God without any consequences, and probably think that the more lies they throw at us, the more we will swallow.

Unfortunately, we're too caught up in life to have the time to research more in depth. The system has been created in such a way to keep us busy all day long. If you don't work overtime, surely, you're heading to your second job or third job, so all you can do when you go home is fall asleep to wake up to another busy day. This happens in school, too. Kids are forced to simply regurgitate information they neither like nor understand, and then, they grow up in a world of facts with no explanation behind them. The same way we have been brought up.

Another awful thing Scientism has taught us is the idea of compromise, for money, of course. This love of money is creeping under our skin, and with it, they managed to corrupt people, who maybe did not even believe in evolution or scientism, but for the sake of comfort and a good life, they decided to trade their morals for a stack of colorful paper.

The case of Dr. Mary Higby Schweitzer, who tested slices of T-Rex bone and discovered elastic tissue and un-fossilized red blood cells, is famous. A creature that supposedly died 65 million years or so ago, had literally active red blood cells. Again, there was no logical explanation from the scientific community. Could Darwin's evolution theory explain this situation? I bet you, it could not, but again, Scientism got into the mix and forcefully pushed that news/idea under the rug.

People have a short memory, right? And if you don't mention anything about a certain event for a while, they will forget about it completely.

Unfortunately for them, we are not all that absent-minded and that's why I return to the idea of creation and intelligent design. They can struggle to hide God's work for as long as they want, but truth has quite a nasty feature: it always tends to come to the surface, regardless of how much you are trying to hide it.

A short chronology of Scientism's ideology:

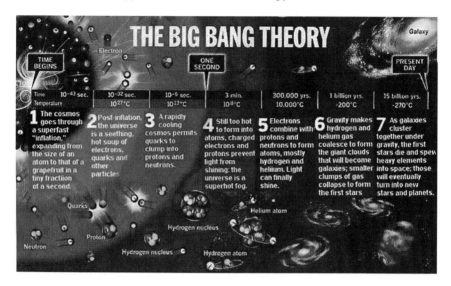

THE BIG BANG THEORY

Galaxy

TIME BEGINS — Electron — ONE SECOND — PRESENT DAY

| Time | 10⁻⁴³ sec. | 10⁻³² sec. | 10⁻⁶ sec. | 3 min. | 300,000 yrs. | 1 billion yrs. | 15 billion yrs. |
| Temperature | | 10²⁷°C | 10¹³°C | 10⁹°C | 10,000°C | -200°C | -270°C |

1 The cosmos goes through a superfast "inflation," expanding from the size of an atom to that of a grapefruit in a tiny fraction of a second.

2 Post-inflation, the universe is a seething, hot soup of electrons, quarks and other particles

3 A rapidly cooling cosmos permits quarks to clump into protons and neutrons.

4 Still too hot to form into atoms, charged electrons and protons prevent light from shining: the universe is a superhot fog.

5 Electrons combine with protons and neutrons to form atoms, mostly hydrogen and helium. Light can finally shine.

6 Gravity makes hydrogen and helium gas coalesce to form the giant clouds that will become galaxies; smaller clumps of gas collapse to form the first stars

7 As galaxies cluster together under gravity, the first stars die and spew heavy elements into space; those will eventually turn into new stars and planets.

Quarks — Neutron — Proton — Hydrogen nucleus — Hydrogen nucleus — Hydrogen atom — Helium atom

20 billion years ago -> the Big Bang (where all the matter in the universe popped up out of nothing in a split second.)

4,6 billion years ago -> the earth cooled down (and then the rain started, and it lasted for millions of years, until the oceans of the earth formed! Where did all that water come from? I am sure it came out of nowhere, too! Clouds just formed by some miracle and that was it.)

After these two major events, the first cell came to life. No one knows for sure how or where it came from, but let's leave it at that. Scientism knows better.

We wouldn't be standing here discussing the theory of evolution of species if Darwin had not gone to the Galapagos islands, where he discovered a considerable variety of finches all having different beaks depending on the island on which they were living. Darwin studied them and reached an outstanding conclusion, that all those finches shared a common ancestor, thus, they must have evolved over the years in some way, up to the point where they had specific characteristics.

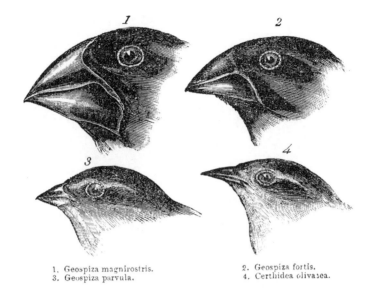

1. Geospiza magnirostris.
3. Geospiza parvula.

2. Geospiza fortis.
4. Certhidea olivasea.

This was the base for his theory, a bunch of birds that looked almost the same, but not quite entirely the same. The theory of evolution was then applied to all living species on earth, the same way that Darwin applied it to those finches in the Galapagos, but he never studied all the species of earth, most of them he did not even know existed. At that time, no one had explored the jungles of the Earth, and that's where you find the greatest variety of species, starting with ants and ending with mammals.

Anyway, if that was not enough, the scientists came up with another idea, that we can determine the evolution of species by analyzing the fossils we find in the dirt. Well, let me tell you, folks, that theory is flawed too, because we might find some bones in the ground, but we have no definitive proof that creature ever had any offspring. As far as we know, its lineage might have ended with it and we keep assuming that it's our common ancestor.

We keep having this **natural selection** stone thrown at us, over and over again, as if this single aspect can solve the evolution equation once and for all. Scientism keeps telling us that natural selection can turn an animal into something else, well, let me break it down for you, Natural selection will only eliminate the bad specimens of a species, the ones that are sick, damaged, and unfit to reproduce, that's all it is. The healthy specimens will carry their genes onward, but it does not mean that they're going to transform into something else just because they managed to stay alive and reproduce. It's not how the game works.

And when you thought it was all over, Scientism finds something

else to throw at you. Maybe they can convince you to believe in their ideas. This time, they came up with the study of **embryos** and they keep trying to explain to us how we are all the same during the first stages of development. From fish to lizard, rat, and human. We must have swum into the primordial ocean, some 500 million years or so ago, because we all have gills.

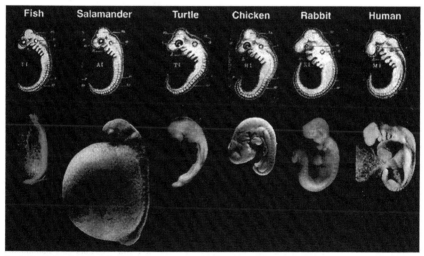

Ernst Haeckel Embryo Fraud

Some might look at the picture and say "Wow, that's it, this is the final proof!" Well, this can happen if you look at the picture with an ignorant eye and zero knowledge or will to research. The pure truth is that those so-called gills are, in fact, the future bones of ears and glands in the throat, so they have nothing to do with breathing underwater... not even 500 million years ago. Also, Ernst Haeckel that tried to convince the world of his finding was later found out to be a fraud and had simply made up the images to further push this evolutionary idea.

Law and Fiction

I bet you did not know, but the Theory of Evolution is the only one defined by law. Yes, you heard it right, defined by law. So, if you choose not to believe in it, because it's clearly a big hoax, you might get in trouble someday. They did this because they feared that someday people might change their minds and decide to go back to the right path, and back to God. These measures they're taking right now actually prove how shallow their doctrine is and how easy it is to disprove, but hey, once they have turned it into law, you can't say no anymore, right? Because it will be against the law.

Right now, there are still close to 50% of Americans who still believe that God created the earth and everything that's on it, somewhere in the last ten thousand years, and it is shocking! Both for those who believe in God, who see how many people have chosen to go to the other side, and for the Scientism followers also, because they can't believe they have not convinced everyone yet! With all the efforts and resources thrown at it, there are still people who know what's true and what's a complete hoax.

This means the game is still on, folks! And they're not going to stop now, not after they struggled for so many decades to take us away from God. Their eyes are still set on our children and they're surely not planning on making any wrong steps from this day on.

Even if they are not adults just yet, the children should have a right to decide what to believe and what to learn, and for that reason, the standard curriculum should have both ideologies. If a child decided to believe the earth is six thousand years old or 4,5 billion years old, it is theirs or their parents' choice. It should not be determined behind closed doors by people who care less about their fate and future.

Members of Scientism called this option of choice "Child abuse", but I believe they are the ones who are abusing our children, by teaching them lies from the earliest ages, when a child cannot really discern between truth and lie and believes, without a doubt, the word of authority (the teacher, in this case).

INDOCTRINATION is the main dish served at our schools today. The kids are not taught how to think, but rather what to think and what to cast aside, preparing them for the same sort of adulthood. Critical thinking is dismissed and, most of the time, they only get to hear only one side of the story, because that fits best with the establishment.

When it comes to the theory of evolution, they should at least learn about the pros and cons of this hypothesis, but instead, they hear only about the fact that it happened and now, we're here! End of story.

Luckily, there are still incredible men in this world who are not afraid, to tell the truth as it is; with no scheming or altering the facts. Joe Taylor from Mt. Blanco Fossil Museum is one of those men, who, through his work over the years, managed to dismantle the evolutionism theories piece by piece and proved that, even with the fossils in his hand, the Biblical approach is still the one that stands up on its feet.

Joe is a passionate paleontologist, who dedicated almost his whole life to exposing the lies of scientism. The evidence he gathered over the years speaks for itself and he's a man who always fought to see the true science put forward.

Joe Taylor Owner of Mt Blanco Fossil Museum

Unfortunately, but as expected, the mainstream science dismissed almost all of Joe's work, including the evidence proving the worldwide flood actually happened, as the Bible says. Scientism cannot accept a different view than theirs, they will not accept, and as a result, they sweep everything under the rug and clean their hands, pretending there was nothing there in the first place.

How carbon (C14) became a miracle

Around the middle of the 20th century, carbon dating was discovered, where, with the help of a specific isotope of carbon (C14, more precisely), scientists could determine the age of fossils with a decent amount of error involved in the process. What are 100,000 years when we are talking about millions and billions here, right?

Well, the truth is that carbon dating only goes a few thousand years back (and even that aspect is disputed by 'scientists'), let alone millions of years, when you find a 'bone turned into stone' and you have absolutely no idea when that creature actually died. It might as well be 10 million years or 100 million years, as no one was there to witness the death.

They say that errors are a human attribute, but when you date the shell of a living snail and it says it's 27,000 years old, you start to wonder if snails can live that long... If you know what I mean.

But let's leave the carbon dating behind, because it's not going to take us anywhere in the end, and let's focus on evolution a little bit and how there are so many fossils in the world (without a giant flood, of course).

We have found skeletons and fossils of creatures from which the living ones today supposedly evolved, but there is a trick here. Darwin 'preached' the survival of the fittest in his books, and yet the fossils suggest a greater complexity than their 'living relatives'. I ask you this now: how can a creature that's perfectly adapted to its environment evolve into a creature that's weaker, smaller, and less adapted? Where is the logic in this, if we are talking about the survival of the fittest?

There are gaps and inconsistencies all over the place, misunderstood discoveries, and sometimes even altered to fit the mainstream scientism. I think that even if we bring them a living dinosaur to stand in front of them to prove that these creatures are not actually millions of years old, they'll say it is not real. Or maybe, they'll say it does not even exist. Who knows?

Right now, we can't even tell for sure if they're extinct at all. We never managed to document all the species living today and we barely scratched the bottom of the oceans, no matter how smart and all-knowing we think we are. So, I believe we should stop giving definitive answers and try to learn more about the world we live in, with the help of true science.

God tells us to seek the truth. God is the ultimate truth in this world and His Word needs to be followed by every living creature, and in the case where Science gets involved, it should align with the Word of God and not fight it to extinction.

Maybe evolution is real, but it does not concern the evolution of species, but the evolution of their tactics and subversive means of taking our identity apart, so they can turn us into mindless sheep in the end, easy to control and to rule. With every passing moment, we're being blinded by those who don't want us to reach the truth anymore.

Chapter 3: Scientism and Dinosaurs

*Can you draw out Leviathan with a fishhook or press down his
tongue with a cord? Can you put a rope in his nose or pierce his
jaw with a hook? Job 41:1*

Translated from the Greek language, Dinosaur means "Ugly
Lizard" and these ugly creatures are supposed to have lived
millions of years ago and were wiped out at some point by a major
cataclysm (a comet that hit near the Yucatan peninsula in the Gulf
of Mexico, at least that is the general theory).

The discovery of the first dinosaur bones in Europe at the end of
17th century represented the start of a new science: paleontology.
There were older accounts of dinosaur bones, especially in China,
right after the birth of Christ. They were calling them Dragon bones,
according to their specific mythology, but they never said those
creatures had lived hundreds and tens of millions of years before.

It is interesting why the English, who discovered the first bones
in a quarry, considered the bones had to be so old, since they had no
way to test that theory. We don't have a viable method of testing the
age of dinosaur bones, even today, since carbon dating can only go
so far back, and the tests aren't always the most conclusive.

At the end of 17th century, Scientism was still in its infancy, but
they knew they needed some 'proof' to demonstrate that they were
right and that the Bible was wrong. Therefore, they came up with
this outrageous idea that dinosaurs lived long before us, thus,
according to those fossils and others, the earth must have been
millions, if not billions, of years old.

The Copernican revolution was unfolding perfectly and it looked
like the evolution theory would fall beautifully on these fossils, and
indeed, dinosaurs have been perceived as the precursors of
mammals, ruling the earth for tens of millions of years, until one

day, when a space rock ended almost everything, because mammals, being smaller and better equipped for harsh environments, managed to survive somehow (eating God knows what, because they said that nothing grew on earth after the comet impacted the surface of our world). If you thought that evolving from monkeys was bad, then look at what Scientism says about the whole mammalian class, okay? Mainstream dogma pretends all mammals, including whales, people, and horses come from some sort of rat, no more than a few inches long, which lived supposedly 25-30 million years ago or more.

Now, let's get back to our dinosaur story and see what actually happened, because the Bible clearly states how the earth is roughly 6000 years old and how God created every living being, including dinosaurs, in this case. The fossils are out there, I have no doubt about that, but what I doubt is their age and how they came to end up in the ground in such great quantities and in some cases, in great concentrations.

Dr. Aaron Judkins

My first stop in this search for the true fate of the dinosaurs was in Glen Rose, Texas, to interview Dr. Aaron Judkins. As an archeologist, he has travelled all over the world, exploring and uncovering many fascinating things. After a while, he realized what was going on on a global scale and tried to shout out to the rest of the world, and for that reason, he has been called many names and is regarded as an unorthodox explorer by the rest of the mainstream science.

With dinosaurs, it matters not what you find in the ground or how conclusive your evidence is. As long as you don't conform to the rest of the mass of scientists, who are supposedly 'holding the truth', then you are considered an outcast and you are pushed aside, until no one remembers your name. Regardless of what dogma says, Aaron is a true scientist and his discoveries have shaken Scientism to its core.

At Glen Rose, Dr. Aaron took me to the site where dinosaur tracks and human footprints lay side by side and it's obvious that they were formed at the same time. I bet you all have the same question in mind that I had when I first saw the tracks. What is the true version?

Did mankind walk on the face of the earth millions of years ago, when dinosaurs supposedly existed or...

Did dinosaurs never go extinct (by a comet) and they managed to live side by side with mankind until recently?

Which one do you think it is?

If you ask me, I strongly believe that God created dinosaurs too, and they lived with us, sharing the earth up to a certain point, when they disappeared, most likely during the great flood that wiped the earth clean of contamination.

PHOTOS BY JEN REEL

A fossil at the Creation Evidence Museum portrays a human footprint under a dinosaur print.

There is no doubt that the tracks at Glen Rose were formed at the same time. The sediments tell that clearly, that's why Scientism could not explain this situation. They tried to say that the human footprints formed later, but it is clear to the naked eye that was impossible, as the sediment is turned into stone now. People could not melt stone 5000 years ago, just so they could make some footprints. That is ridiculous, and yet that was Scientism's best explanation.

The fact is that, at the normal rate of erosion, the tracks at Glen Rose should not have existed at all, since the river bed should have been 5 feet lower than the current level. I say this, because mainstream scientists claim the traces must be at least 150 million years old. And yet, there is no sign of evident erosion, not at that level at least. The tracks are fresh, and you can clearly observe the edges, meaning that they are much more recent... Unbelievably recent!

Comparing mainstream scientists and archeologists with Dr. Aaron, I immediately spotted a huge difference that convinced me instantly. In the case of other archeologists, the sites are closed to the large public, but Dr. Aaron invites any volunteers who want to perform some real excavation yearly. Why does this happen? Well, let me tell you the secret. Main stream archeologists are under strict supervision and those people who finance and control the projects are afraid for their discoveries and don't want anything to leak to the masses. If they find something controversial, it will end up somewhere in some dark basement and will never see the light of day.

The world is supposed to know only what they consider fit for the world to know. The level of conspiracy and censorship in archeology is absolutely frightening, and that's why we rarely find out about some outstanding discoveries. It does not mean that archeologists don't find things in the ground. The truth is that they are signing non-disclosure contracts, which prevent them from telling the world about their findings.

What is the purpose of science and archeology then, I dare to ask? Just so an occult minority could control all the means and information, so in the end, they can control the world? This scenario is closer to truth than to fiction, trust me.

Even the Bible mentions the dragons, as one of God's mightiest creations, so it is obvious that dinosaurs lived among men, at the same time with men:

"Behold now behemoth, which I made with thee; he eateth grass as an ox. Lo now, his strength is in his loins, and his force is in the navel of his belly. He moveth his tail like a cedar: the sinews of his stones are wrapped together. His bones are as strong pieces of brass; his bones are like bars of iron. He is the chief of the ways of God: he that made him can make his sword to approach unto him. Surely the mountains bring him forth food, where all the beasts of the field play. He lieth under the shady trees, in the covert of the reed, and fens. The shady trees cover him with their shadow; the willows of the brook compass him about. Behold, he drinketh up a river, and hasteth not: he trusteth that he can draw up Jordan into his mouth. He taketh it with his eyes: his nose pierceth through snares." Job 40: 15-24

This is a clear description of a Sauropod dinosaur, as no other large land herbivore fits this exact description. No hippo, elephant, or anything else would ever have a cedar-like tale, but then again, to scientism, this is impossible, since it did not happen 100 million years ago.

Dinosaur is a new name for a creature existent in all the world's mythologies and histories. We can find accounts of the same creature, under different names, all around the world. The vocabulary does not lie, and people had no reason to talk about and describe a creature they had never seen in their life.

Here are just a few names for dinosaurs (dragon):

Tineen- Arabic	Dragon- English	Dragon- French
Balaur- Romanian	Draak- Dutch	Drache- German
Drakon- Bulgarian	Drage- Danish	

And the list goes on and on, as each civilization mentions this mythical creature and how mighty it was, compared to the rest of the creatures in the animal kingdom. Since people talked about it, it would be safe to assume that dinosaurs are a much more recent species and did not go extinct at the end of the Jurassic era, but scientism insists in telling us that those fossils we find in the ground are millions of years old. With all the evidence in front of their eyes, the propaganda keeps going on the established path.

We all know the films and cartoons portraying dinosaurs, from the Flintstones to Jurassic Park, and all the other smaller cartoons that depict dinosaurs as friendly creatures and not those bloody, giant beasts, able to kill anything in their path (at least the carnivores). We can see cartoons where even the T-Rex, the most vicious dinosaur ever excavated, is portrayed as a friendly folk to kids. This is, again, an example of preemptive programming to get the idea of dinosaurs stuck into children's brains.

Now, let's get back to T-Rex a bit, and see how they never really excavated a full body and yet, we see skeletons in museums all over the world. They find a tooth and some vertebra, and they imagine how the animals must have looked. Again, simple suppositions that we should take as facts and hold them in high esteem as the ultimate truth. What they are doing is guesswork and a bad job of it at that.

When I saw Jurassic Park for the first time, I could not stop laughing, until I lost my breath. How they told people they found a mosquito in amber, hundreds of millions of years old, and which had 'fresh' DNA inside it.

Jurassic Park movie logo and mosquito in amber.

First of all, DNA does not survive for so long, regardless of what methods you use, (and I know for sure they did not have fridges, millions of years ago).

Then, let's say, the mosquito thing really works, and you can extract the much-needed DNA. In the film, they had lots of dinosaurs, both herbivores and carnivores, plus flying ones, and they did not all live during the same era (according to the dogma), then how did they extract the DNA for so many species from only one mosquito? Did that poor insect collect blood from dozens of dinosaurs? How did it do it, anyway? Suck some blood from a dinosaur, then hibernate for 10-20 million years, wake up and suck some more blood and then hibernate again for another 20 million years, waiting for the next species to evolve?

The whole idea is absurd, but the purpose of the movie was not to present true scientific facts. The goal was to imprint those images into people's heads and it worked too, because kids nowadays can hardly recognize an eggplant, but if you ask them about a T-Rex or Stegosaurus, they have so much to tell you about it.

Scientists kept talking so much about dinosaurs and said so many lies, but by doing it consistently, they fooled everyone into thinking that mainstream archeologists really knew what they were talking about! They had no idea what they were saying, but it did not stop them, as they were not looking for the truth, but for fame and money.

Dinosaurs existed, but not 100 million years ago. They were breathing the same air as the ancient man and people saw them in flesh and bones. We can see depictions of dinosaurs carved in stones and columns and buildings of ancient civilizations and you could not believe how detailed those carvings are. I mean, they even got the number of scales correctly... How would scientists explain this? We all know that civilizations in South and Central America are no older than 2500 years, and yet, they have drawings of dinosaurs. Following a mainstream science judgment, we should conclude that such beasts wandered through the lands at least 2500 years ago, if not closer to the present day.

What does scientism say about these proofs? Well, they kind of ignore them, saying such a thing is impossible, and yet, the drawings are vivid. The ancients could not have found a bone and constructed the rest starting from that. They did not have computers or 3D simulation technology, so they saw exactly what they were drawing with their own eyes.

Everything scientists can't explain regarding dinosaur findings, and this happens with everything else that does not fit the description, they regard it as metaphorical expressions of ancient man. As if people were dreaming of dinosaurs during the night and, in the morning, they started chipping stone, without knowing exactly what they were drawing. This does not happen. People have always drawn and carved the things existing in their environment, and this was their way of immortalizing their world for 'eternity'.

Why aren't scientists claiming the same things about the cave paintings in France, Spain, and everywhere else, where bulls, deer, and other common hunting animals were painted on the walls of the caves? We know those animals existed in that period, so there is no danger for disclosure. Shortly said, it is not dangerous for the current establishment.

The dinosaur debate is still controversial, and there are countless

examples where things don't add up, and the fossils archeologists find in the ground can't explain their own existence. We have a narrow etymology and a narrow mind when judging the facts and relics we uncover, and that's preventing us from seeing the truth. This

Stegosaurus carving at 800-year-old Ta Prohm Temple in Cambodia.

happens mainly because we have been forced and programmed to believe only a single set of coordinates that are not always taking us to the truth.

When we find something that does not fit the current dogma, archeologists simply throw it away and search until they find something that can be 'approved'. Instead of adapting our theories to our findings, we adapt our findings to our rigid and sometimes erroneous theories. This is a completely flawed judgment, meant to set us away from the truth and Word of God. The Creator keeps sending us clues and we keep throwing them under the rug. For how long, I keep wondering…

Chapter 4: Scientism and the Universe

Canst thou bind the sweet influences of Pleiades, or loose the bands of Orion? Job 38:31

The Universe is the oldest, most complex structure we have ever known. With a lifespan of over 20 billion years, and in continued expansion even as we speak, the universe is so complex and vast, that our human minds can barely comprehend it. And it's obvious why it is so hard for us to understand this universe, since it's a new concept for us. Throughout our history, humanity had different views about the world and how things work. We saw the earth as being flat and having a firmament that protected us from any danger, and then, all of a sudden, the 'glass dome' shattered and we were thrown into a spinning game around a regular sun, at the edge of a regular galaxy, in a Universe that simply has no boundaries.

No wonder people started feeling small and insignificant in the face of this ageless giant that is the Universe!

The ancients knew that all the stars, planets, and even the sun were hanging from the firmament, and they assumed there had to be a God or gods, who were responsible for their creation and the creation of the world. For thousands of years, their beliefs went unchallenged, until the middle ages, when scientists decided to change the paradigm and place the sun in the center of the 'universe', instead of earth.

This sacrilege was based on mere assumptions and no actual proofs, but slowly, it took roots in the minds of people. The era of science fiction had started hundreds of years ago and not in the 20th century, as people might assume.

Right now, we're living in an age where science and science-fiction are practically the same. The driving force of this process is not repeated testing and observation anymore, but rather, the mad scientist's imagination, which looks like it might have no limits. Just think about it for a moment, right now, the 'scientists' decide what we should believe first, and then, they try to come up with the math to fit with their agenda. It's not testing, observing, and proving anymore! Now they decide upon a 'universal truth' and then, they make up some sort of 'logical' explanation.

Enormous black holes, gravitational waves, quasars, and the list could go on forever. Things we never saw with our own eyes and never managed to prove their existence in the first place, and yet, they are a part of the scientific dogma. Doesn't this make you wonder how come they fooled us so easily into believing their nonsense? These people will admit the snow is black, even if you show it to them to be white, and yet, the same people come up with theories and ideas that have no concrete backing... And all with just one purpose in mind: to exclude God from the bigger picture.

Even top scientists admitted, in their attempts to solve the mysteries of the Universe, how their theories resembled the way the Kabbalah explains the origins of life and the universe. The ancient, pagan teaching falls hand in hand with the current scientific dogma of the endless universe and the Big Bang theory.

Sir Isaac Newton, the father of gravity, is known to have had access to mystical writings and documents (including Zohar and Kabbalah), and he was not the only one in this situation. This fact should draw a question mark in everyone's mind, because it looks like science did not actually start as science, but rather as a hidden agenda.

When the Bible states the truth about the sun, moon, and stars inside the firmament of the earth, this means it has to be this way. God's Word will always be the truth and truth will always come to light. That's why we see so much effort put into convincing us that we live in an endless cosmos, on a spinning, pale blue dot.

The Bible says that God himself sits on the firmament in all His glory and that, one day, all the stars shall fall to earth. Well, if someone could please explain to me how stars that are billions and billions of light years away will fall to earth, while the universe keeps expanding (this means those stars are getting away from us as we speak)? Not to mention, that all the stars are supposed to be, in fact, multitudes bigger than Earth, so how are we going to cram all those fiery balls together, huh?

The notion of God creating the world and everything else in six days might sound absurd to many, but then, I ask you again, how we can believe Scientism's statements, when they admit, with their own mouths, how their margin of error can be up to 96%? I mean, isn't it ludicrous to

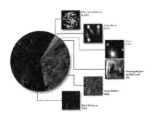

Observational evidence?

state that you have no idea if what you're saying is actually true, but at the same time to demand that the world should believe your nonsense?

On the other hand, the Bible does not make assumptions or educated guesses. In Genesis, we're told exactly when and what God created. It is right there under our noses, and all we have to do is read it! At first, God created the heavens and the earth, and then he made the sun, the moon, and the stars... And there, everything ends, where the Universe is concerned. The Bible does not talk about any distant planets that might or might not be able to sustain life as we know it.

The scientists are selling us their assumption of a planet anyway, because they can't actually see the planets that are dozens of lights years away, or how Carl Sagan would like to say, billions and billions and billions of millions of miles away. The only thing the scientists can see through their powerful telescopes is a twinkling star. That's it, and they can't even see it that well. And from that foggy image, they start theorizing and yelling that they have discovered some wonderful, new planet, that is even better than Earth. They name something they have never seen and have no actual certainty that it exists at all.

I bet you might be thinking about Mars, Venus, and all the other planets of the 'solar system' right now. Well, let me tell you this, in the book of Enoch, these celestial bodies are mentioned under the name: Wandering Stars, so there's no mentioning of the word 'planet'. According to the Bible, except the sun and the moon, the rest of them are all stars, nothing else.

The 21st century is the age of speed and overwhelming information. With the help of the internet, we have access to vast amounts of information, and there comes the tricky part. As with everything in this world, there is good information and bad information, there is truth and there is deception out there. For regular folks, it might be a bit difficult to filter so much information and determine what's fact and what's fake. For that reason, we all need to go back to the ultimate source of truth. Any good Christian knows the Bible is the source of that truth, the Word of God, and we need to read and understand, and then, with the help of that knowledge, we can filter all those gigabytes of information we find on the web.

There are deceivers out there, who want to capture our attention with their lies, and they want to make us believe their version of the 'truth'. You'll find countless documentaries and 'scientific papers' trying to lure you into their trap.

How do you feel when you hear Scientism apostates like Richard Dawkins calling God "The most unpleasant character of all fiction, jealous and proud of it, a petty unjust, unforgiving control-freak; a vindictive, bloodthirsty ethnic cleanser, a misogynistic, homophobic, racist, infanticidal, genocidal, filicidal, pestilential, megalomaniacal, sadomasochistic capriciously malevolent bully?" What's the sensation you get when witnessing their ignorance, as they keep calling God "An ever-receding pocket of scientific ignorance?"

Or what about Lawrence Krauss saying, "Forget Jesus, the stars died so you could be born." They say blasphemous statements like this, because Scientism is now claiming that we are all made up of stardust, the result of terrible explosions that happened millions, or maybe billions, of years ago and now we're here. These crazy scientists keep saying these things, with a big smile on their face, as if they reached some sort of revelation. They think that they finally managed to grasp the ultimate truth, when, in fact, they could not be farther from it.

God did not create the earth, the sun, and the stars... No, they just created themselves under the guidance of some strange 'laws' that have been here forever, and all formed from something that popped up out of nowhere and out of nothing. This is Scientism's strongest theory, the origin of everything, and they make it look like we are the ones who are crazy for not believing their fantasy.

If we are nothing but stardust, a set of chemicals resulting from great supernovas, what brought that dust to life? Did it come alive all by itself, the same way the planets and the stars came into being? To me, the more I ask myself these questions, the more illogical their theory becomes.

At a closer examination, we can observe that Scientism is very spiritual in nature, despite its claims. Its main goal is to destroy people's belief in the Bible's account of the creation of everything, to cast doubt into people's hearts, and to shatter God's credibility in people's eyes.

As mentioned earlier, the idea of evolutionism, the Big Bang, and the vast universe did not begin with Darwin and the enlightenment, but it has deeper roots in ancient history around the Mediterranean Sea and the Middle East. Satan worked with different, powerful men over the ages, in order to impose an ideology. Starting with Ancient Egyptian, Ancient Greek, and Babylonian mystery schools, we can observe the prevalence of the all-powerful and all-knowing humanity. We see how they have tried to take God out of the equation so many times before.

All we have witnessed so far leads us to one conclusion. Their final goal was to rewrite history, erase creationism from people's minds, and make them forget about God Almighty, so that, in the end, they themselves could pose as gods and rule over the earth. If there is no other hope, people tend to accept almost anything. If their minds are poisoned with doubt, they'll keep their heads down and never raise them to look up at the sky.

Yes, up there, there is the most visible and greatest deception of all time, because if we can't really see fossils, except in museums (and God knows what happened to them until they got there and if they are real at all, since most of them are reconstructions, based mostly on guessing), then we can surely gaze at the stars, and we can see them moving above our heads.

For thousands of years, we all agreed that the earth stood still, while everything else moved above our heads, including the Sun and the Moon. But then Copernicus decided to change the paradigm and took the earth from the middle of the universe and placed it somewhere around a random, mediocre star (the sun).

John Calvin called those who proposed the earth was moving as being possessed by the devil, bitter, wicked minds, whose only goal was to poison the minds of others, and make them go against the natural order of things. This man knew exactly what was going on five hundred years ago.

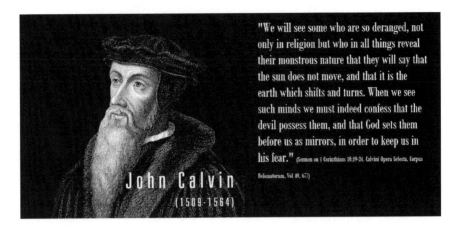

"We will see some who are so deranged, not only in religion but who in all things reveal their monstrous nature that they will say that the sun does not move, and that it is the earth which shifts and turns. When we see such minds we must indeed confess that the devil possess them, and that God sets them before us as mirrors, in order to keep us in his fear." (Sermon on 1 Corinthians 10:19-24. Calvini Opera Selecta, Corpus Reformatorum, Vol 49, 677)

John Calvin (1509-1564)

The assault on the Bible came under different forms and on different fronts. Friedrich Nietzsche, one of the fathers of modern philosophy, cheerfully stated the death of God and the beginning of the Copernican revolution and supported the work of Roger Boscovich, a Jesuit philosopher.

"For while Copernicus convinced us to believe, contrary to all our senses, that the earth did not stand still, Boscovich taught us to renounce the belief in the final thing which made the earth "stand firm," the belief in "stuff," in "material," in what was left of the earth, in atomic particles. It was the greatest triumph over the senses which has ever been achieved on earth so far. But we must go even further and also declare war, a relentless war to the bitter end, against the "atomistic need," which still carries on a dangerous afterlife in places where no one suspects, like that celebrated "metaphysical need."

This so-called revolution was a breakthrough by the Scientism agenda and, through their force, they managed to perpetuate it and transform it into such a phenomenon, that it basically outshined everything else within society. This was the single most preeminent 'discovery' that shadowed the medieval Christianity and shook the old establishment to its roots. A single individual, with one theory, succeeded in dethroning a theocratic mentality, thus preparing the new dogma and mentality for the ages to come.

The spark that fired this revolution was represented by the introduction of the so-called Copernican principle, which was defined from the beginning as a 'working assumption' that arose from a modified cosmological extension of Copernicus' heliocentric universe. This principle stated that neither the sun nor the earth were in a specially favored position in the universe, thus we're living on a regular piece of stone, floating through the space around a regular star. Close to the present day, this principle has been extended, as we are not considered to be privileged observers of the universe anymore.

I keep thinking why these people insisted so much on trying to make humanity look so unimportant. What did they have to gain out of it? I just can't see it, regardless of how hard I look and then I got back to John Calvin and his statement, where he said they must have been possessed by the Devil.

God let us know that we and our home, the Earth, we are His ultimate creation, God's pride. This made humanity unique and gave it meaning, a purpose in life, and we all knew why we were breathing and living in this world.

Scientism and the 'scientific community' agree that this so-called Copernican Revolution, which sparked the scientific advancements of the Renaissance and Enlightenment in Europe, is based on the pre-conceived cosmological assumptions of helio-centrism and a massive, isotropic universe.

Keep this word in mind, "Assumption," because you're going to see it a lot more from now on. It looks like our world, the 'scientific world,' and all the laws and theories that are supposed to govern our lives, are based on assumptions, and, at the end of the day, an assumption is nothing but an assumption.

True science should be backed only by objective evidence alone. Doubt and assumptions should never be a part of the scientific process, unless you are trying to create something else and decide to call it "science." Anyway, we'll talk more in detail about it later.

Now, let's go back to our endless universe, where we are nothing but a speck of dust, meant to disappear one day, forever.

Speaking of fading away completely, it is worth mentioning that Copernicus' theories and ideas are hiding a different purpose, a different philosophy that is easily negligible to an untrained eye. Embedded in the Copernican principle, there is a more implicit philosophical assumption, one that regards everything and everyone breathing in this universe. Now, the implications are more significant and more reaching than one might assume, and at closer inspection, this half-millennium old principle underlines and expresses a philosophy we all recognize all around us today: Materialism.

You may be a little bit confused right now, so let me break it down for you and explain things a little bit more in depth. This philosophical concept was slipped in so cleverly and so covertly, probably knowing that, over the years, it would take root in people's subconsciousness.

Copernicus' principle assumes that the universe looks the same, regardless of the point in space from where you look at it, and that the earth holds no special place inside that same universe. Based on that same principle, one must deduce that the Universe is categorically and qualitatively homogenous, thus measurable, according to specific means and laws. The conclusion? The whole universe is strictly material, and we, as a part of it, are strictly material too. We don't have a soul anymore, we're just flesh and bone, ready to rot as soon as we draw our last breath.

What the adepts of the Copernican Revolution wanted to achieve with us was a degrading of our self-worth. They tried to make us regress mentally to the stage of animals, where we could mingle with them, become indistinguishable. God's ultimate creation was to become, in their eyes, no more than a beast.

We see how people deeply involved in Scientism kept telling us that we should leave Earth behind and look for another home, because this one is not sustainable anymore. They keep shouting that we should colonize Mars or some distant, frozen moon we had not seen in our lives and probably does not exist at all.

I have not seen a more blasphemous urge in my life. God has created the Earth for us, so we could live on it and prosper, the perfect Garden, beautiful and balanced, and where a man can find everything he needs without too much effort and struggle. Why do they want to separate us from our home, when we all know there is no other home out there for us? Why are they seeding this doubt inside our heads and making us think that we 'appeared' on Earth by coincidence and could have appeared some other place as easily or we could not have appeared at all?

Is it that, maybe, this is a desperate attempt in which they're trying to cut our roots and make our feeling of belonging and property fade away, so that, one day, when we will least expect it, we'll hear, "This isn't your home anymore, the Earth Is Ours!"?

The heavens, even the heavens, are the LORD'S: but the earth hath he given to the children of men. Psalm 115:16

The way Scientism began to infiltrate and spread, might have seemed, to most Christians, as nothing wrong, since figures such as Isaac Newton were perceived as god-fearing Christians, who were helping scientific advancement and human knowledge. The truth is that he and other 'scientists', such as Copernicus and Keppler, shared rather atheistic worldviews, and the masses knew nothing about their true doctrines and convictions.

Gradually, Newton and others were building up and strengthening the materialistic philosophy. The doctrine saying that everything in the world and universe must be quantifiable and measurable, according to certain sets of rules and laws, would have further ramifications that would shock the world.

It is unknown if Newton and his fellows had any idea about the hidden and unforeseen developments that were going to take place later in time. If they planned for this to happen or not has not yet been determined, but we still have time to investigate, thus nothing is lost.

What we know for a fact, instead, is how all the physical science became dominated by this materialistic paradigm, eventually. With laws and principles and equations more or less accurate, more or less precise, this discipline was drowning in materialism, and it looked like Scientism needed to find another target in order to fulfill its agenda. And what could be a better choice than to play with the living world?

'The Universe' was theirs now, cold and inanimate, they could not touch or feel it, so all they had to do was suppose and guess, presume and hope, but now things were different. Life was God's greatest creation, the cherry on top of the cake, and scientism knew that. They were aware that, in order to 'conquer' people's hearts and minds, they had to dominate all living, breathing creatures.

If you think that Darwin and his theories have nothing to do with Copernicus and Newton and their studies of the Universe and laws of physics, then I must tell you that you are wrong and that you need to open your eyes and realize this was a concerted effort sharing the same agenda. They are all linked together, because they all share the same end goal, and that's the subjugation of the human race and to distort the reality of God's creation by destroying the foundation of the Bible.

Looking further in time at the development of certain social and behavioral philosophies, deriving from the same materialistic central idea (humanism/ communism), we can observe the same attempt at creating an image of the universe on earth, a homogenous mass, with no distinct features, and where God really has no place.

This fake idea where Man is in the center of everything, while, in fact, he was not in the center of anything at all, corrupted millions and killed millions. A sort of sick experiment that played with people's minds and souls and stripped their souls of any virtue by playing with their most inner fears and desires.

This amorphous entity we got to call Scientism, spread through the Christian world faster than a plague, managing to infect and infiltrate the Christian community, the church, and the family, creating gaps and disputes between people. They worked by separating people, as they were easier to control and brainwash. Copernicus and his helio-centric theories serve as a Trojan horse for the rest of Scientisms' philosophies, as it helped to break the Christian wall, so that the flood of new, unholy ideas and concepts could come upon the people.

Darwinism and Copernican principles cannot be separated as distinct ideas, because, on a deep subconscious level, they are perceived as symbiotic elements that can't really exist if taken apart. These two ideologies acted as a foundation for all the theories and speculations that followed, regarding the Universe and humanity's place in it. Eventually, it all turned into a monolith so huge and so well-structured that it seems impossible to break or dismantle.

Fortunately, people have started thinking for themselves lately, and more people are beginning to doubt the 'orthodox scientific dogma'. I am sure that, soon, we will reach a point in history thought to be inconceivable and we will prove how Scientism was based on false premises, proposed by such giants as Newton, Galileo, and Einstein. The fathers of modern science did nothing else but build their theories and assumptions on the same philosophy: Copernicanism, a deeply rooted, corrupted attempt at separating mankind from its creator.

Chapter 5: Scientism and the Occult

The secret which the king hath demanded cannot the wise men, the astrologers, the magicians, the soothsayers, shew unto the king;
Daniel 2:27

If we look back in history, we can see how human society has been plagued by all sorts of occult groups and practices, people who were trying to hide certain truths and concepts from the rest of the population. Even today, we have a great number of 'secret' societies, such as the Illuminati, the Freemasons, the Skulls and Bones, but they are not so secret anymore, because they managed to induce this idea to the rest of the people that they are doing nothing wrong.

And yet, we only get to know their names, because everything else besides their names is shrouded in mystery. Their occult practices and philosophies are concealed from the large public and they only appear now and then, smiling to our faces.

The word "Occult" itself is repugnant by nature. The term *occult* (from the Latin word *occultus* "clandestine, hidden, secret") is knowledge of the hidden, the secrecy it proposes, the scheming and the shadows make it unnatural, unwanted. Still, people colluded with this dark spirituality, adopted it, and even turned it into a lifestyle. They who were most involved with the occult considered the rest of the people as lesser beings, unworthy of knowing what they knew, thus only worthy of being ruled and commanded. A rule that did not share any principles and only bits and crumbs of information, enough to make the people awe.

To define the 'occult' phenomenon, we need to start off with Pythagoras, who, in a sense, can be considered the father of occultism with Scientism. He lived in the most advanced society in

Europe at the time, but this does not explain his breakthroughs in mathematics and other fields of 'science'.

Pythagoras Greek philosopher

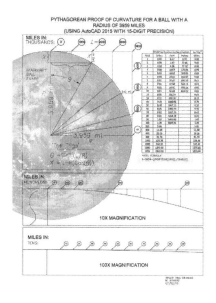

Upon further analysis, I realized Pythagoras' deep connection with the Egyptian world, which shared even deeper secrets and occult knowledge. The deeper I went down in history, the harder it was for me to explain how certain members of society (the ruling class, in general) knew things that were basically impossible to know in their time.

Anyway, let's get back to Pythagoras and his most famous 'discovery', the Pythagorean Theorem, a basic principle of mathematics that helped develop the rest of Science. In fact, even when calculating the curvature of the Earth we use Pythagoras' theorem (8 inches per mile square).

Upon further research and analysis, I realized that Pythagoras was, in fact, nothing but a normal man, who did not actually discover things naturally, but rather by spiritual means. Men aren't capable of creating such elaborate theories, such as the Big Bang or the origin of life (evolution). They come from a dark force that has been in rebellion with God since day one and is working with men to bring upon his new world order.

This led me back to mystery schools, the occult, and how Pythagoras realized their importance in understanding the world. Thus, because of his 'thirst' for knowledge, Pythagoras began traveling to Egypt, as mentioned earlier, but also to other areas of the known world, where he knew that he would find ancient cultures he could learn from. He understood that knowledge cannot be 'invented,' but only experienced through the ages, learned by error and trial, thus, for a number of years, he traveled around the world, gathered the information, analyzed it, and in the end, he turned it into a discipline: Philosophy which had numbers as its cornerstone.

He viewed numbers as the fundamental elements of creation, the only way to understand divinity and the world he lived in. If you take a break and look around you with a keen eye, you'll realize that we're surrounded by mathematical constants like 'Pi', the speed of light, the force of gravity as proposed by Newton, so it would look like the world is indeed governed by numbers, but is it?

Pythagoras' goal was to produce other philosophers like himself, but his school was not actually for everyone. He'd choose his students personally and only those with certain mental traits would be admitted. I wondered why Pythagoras concealed his knowledge, revealing it to only a select few. If his ideas were indeed so brilliant and so groundbreaking, it's safe to say that the whole world should benefit, right?

Soon, Pythagoras turned the Babylonian numerical system into a secret science, in his attempt to reach divinity. To him, a number was like God, and thus, the safest way to get in contact with the same God, and yet with all his acquired 'wisdom', Pythagoras could never get in touch with God, as God can't be reduced to a number. Their lack of understanding of God's ways led them astray from the true paths.

Their failure and bitterness pushed them away from God, and Pythagoras' science evolved over the years into numerology, Kabbalah, and other secret 'sciences', which were supposed to offer their followers great insight.

So, thousands of years ago, Pythagorean mysticism reduced everything to numbers, the same homogenous mass as in the case of Copernicus, where everything can be measured, calculated, and thus defined in one way or another.

Now, take a moment and think about the world we live in today. Does it ring a bell? The age of information, where everything can be reduced to ones and zeros? In our so-called digital age, factual math is so dependable, so exact, so capable of producing technological marvels, that people have all the reasons to believe in something that is mathematically supportable.

The technological 'awe' has blinded most of us and rendered us indifferent to the reality that stands behind the numbers, because it's never going to be just numbers, there's always something else behind them. While math has grown into being considered an exact, objective science that never fails, the truth is that even numbers can have a subjective aura, a degree of occult spiritism around them.

We heard these words too many times: Numbers Never Lie! And what if they do? What if these numbers we praise so much are, in fact, the greatest lie we've ever been fed, under the disguise of objectivity?

It's hard to believe this, right? After all, we've all been raised to worship and venerate science and math for their exactness, for their objectivity. When everything else fails, numbers will save us. We keep believing that science and math are two objective tools in the hands of the elite, used solely for the betterment of humankind.

And most of us believed it when they kept claiming that science rises above all those machinations of the world, such as religion or philosophy, that science is something completely different, something that cannot be corrupted or tainted by human flaws, as if science was God itself.

Again, I feel it is my duty to remind all of you that everything in this world has been created by humans, everything except for the Bible, which is the Word of God. The rest is our word, our ideas, and interpretations, and this is subject to error, to malevolent planning and scheming. Think twice when you hear again that Science and mathematics are dedicated to finding the truth and only the truth. If these tools are wielded by people, at least a small amount of doubt should always be there.

People's actions will always be dictated by their interests, their speeches will be transformed by what they need, and when you expect less, you see them changing their faces. This is the nature of man.

God's Word is immovable, it does not change, it has not changed, and it will stay like this until the end of days.

These occult societies are fully aware of this truth, and since they could not reach God, they tried through various means to take us away from Him. Just look at their mockery, pretending to use science to help the world, but at the same time, they laugh, saying they could not find God in Space.

Through the occult societies, a thought was propagated: that we are gods! This sense of entitlement, a feeling of superpower that takes away any responsibility from people, is both malign and poisonous.

We might be smart, smarter than anything else that has ever walked the Earth, but we should never forget who the Creator is. God made us intelligent, because he wanted to give us a different sense of perception, a consciousness to help us understand the real meaning of life. He did not create us in his image, so we could bask in our own pool of pride and ignorance, but then again, we can decide for ourselves, even if sometimes we're not making the best decisions.

Chapter 6: Scientism and the Heavens

(The Heliocentric vs Geocentric Debate)

In them hath he set a tabernacle for the sun. Which is as a bridegroom coming out of his chamber, and rejoiceth as a strong man to run a race. Psalm 19:3-4

A few years ago, if you were to ask a kindergarten child about the earth and the solar system, he would certainly have told you that the earth is the 3rd planet from the sun in a system of 9 planets. Today, we learn that there are only 8, because Pluto has been disqualified from the game, for some reason... Even they can't agree with their ludicrous ideas.

Anyway, the Bible describes quite clearly the arrangement of the earth, the sun, the moon, and the stars and the relation between them. It is easy to understand and rather logical for all those who want to see.

There is the earth, the clouds, the sky, then there's the firmament that's protecting us, holding the waters from above; and then, the heavens of heavens, where God resides watching over us.

The key point in this equation was that the Earth was stationary and everything else moved around it. Ptolemy's geostationary theory worked for over 1500 years, astronomy and viable calendars were created following that pattern; everything worked perfectly until one day, when Scientism decided it was all over. Nicolas Copernicus detested Ptolemy's discovery and was set on turning everything upside down.

His theories of heliocentrism soon penetrated the universities and other centers of knowledge and education, and in a matter of years, he managed to gradually break the back of Bible credibility as the ultimate source of truth in Christendom. Over the last few centuries, intense propaganda has managed to batter the covers of the Bibles and the image in people's minds that the earth might be stationary.

Geocentric vs. Heliocentric

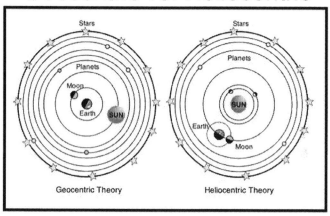

Geocentric vs. Heliocentric Model

There are certainly people who don't even know that such theories existed in the first place. So raw and effective was Scientism's propaganda that it managed to wipe out crucial information on a collective level. The scientific priesthood, with its radical members, battled the truth relentlessly in their effort to converge people on a world scale towards their version of the story and make them think that it's okay to believe that the earth is spinning at thousands of miles per hour around its axis and around the sun at the same time and we would not feel any effect.

Once this was achieved, they knew it would be easier for them to convince everyone that we were not created by God. With no creation, there was no need for heaven, there wouldn't be any temptation from Satan, no guilt, no need for Jesus to lift us from damnation, thus no need for God at all. With this heliocentric system in our hands, we had nothing above our heads beyond air and space... No one to watch and hold us accountable for our deeds... We were the masters of our own destiny.

The Bible clearly states how the Firmament is made up of a solid material, transparent, but solid like transparent glass, so if I may ask these clever 'astronauts' and scientists, how do their rockets pierce through it to go to 'space'? Or is this just another elaborate hoax to fool people into believing we are spinning around the sun?

Fortunately, not everyone was convinced by Copernicus' theories, and the greatest astronomer of that time, the illustrious Danish nobleman, Tycho Brahe, developed a new geocentric model, where the earth occupies the center like in the Ptolemaic model. The difference, in this case, was the fact that the planets orbited the sun, while the sun orbited around the earth.

Tycho's observations were accurate and very precise for long periods of time, proving his theory to be correct against Copernicus' claims. In fact, the Sun is traveling around the Earth, causing the ecliptic orbit and not the other way around. The sun's movement also generates the seasons and all the changes taking place in our atmosphere.

At that time, the dispute between Copernicus's adepts and Tycho's theories was fierce, as Copernicans could not accept another version, regardless of the fact that they were perpetrating a lie. They would not just stand and watch as all their efforts went to ruin.

So, it happened, that Tycho Brahe hired a young apprentice, of the name Johannes Kepler, in 1600. Instead of learning and helping his employer, Keppler began working on his own development of the Copernican system. Unfortunately, he needed Tycho's observations to succeed in developing his theory, but Tycho Brahe refused to help him in any way.

Fortune made it that, in 1601, Tycho Brahe died suddenly. No one could tell the actual cause of death, so Kepler remained in charge of all Tycho's observations (quite convenient, isn't it?) and used them to develop his own system. Therefore, over the ages, Kepler remained known as one of the greatest astronomers the world had ever seen. We even named our deep space telescope after him, while Tycho Brahe's name faded in history and only those passionate about astronomy remember him and his achievements.

It's weird how at crucial points in time, when certain people, great men, are trying to reveal the scheme and show the world the truth, they simply disappear. So conveniently that those remaining behind have the last word and tell us what the 'dead man' wanted to say. This way, they manage to distort the truth and use the efforts that were directed initially against the scientism agenda and against the greatest deception mankind has ever seen.

With Brahe's observations in his hands, Kepler developed a theory, which suggested that the sun must play a crucial role in the rotation of the planets. His insight was decisive and noticed how the planets followed very definite paths, and Kepler suggested that the Sun was responsible for their movement. The sun kept them in rotation and the further a planet was from the sun, the weaker its force upon that planet.

In Kepler's system, the planets did not move circularly anymore, but rather in ellipses, non-uniformly. The ellipsis, with its two flocci, allows us to observe Ptolemy's epicycles as a brilliant attempt to express no uniform motion, hundreds of years before Kepler was even born.

So, once the idea of no-uniform motion was introduced, all these systems could be portrayed as geometrically identical.

Now, if we investigate the textbooks in our schools, we'll see that Kepler was, in fact, a Christian; a man with a fear of God, who was doing God's work, so we should not be suspicious about anything in his case. Luckily, I am too old for this kind of charade and I know with certainty that there's always more than meets the eye, therefore, I always decide to dig further to get my hands on the actual truth.

After analyzing Kepler's work and theology, I realized that he wasn't the regular type of a Biblical Christian. His writings and research proved him to be concerned by different matters than the Word of God. His use of the doctrine of accommodation and his reliance on what philosophy and science call the 'Book of Nature' seemed to always work for the benefit of Kepler.

The Book of Nature is not actually a paperback thing you can touch with your hand, but rather a philosophical concept, an abstract idea, something that was supposed to govern people's lives. Emerging sometime in the 14th century, the Book of Nature concept is supposed to be a synthesis of ideologies and precepts, related to the study of nature and understanding of life through nature. One of the main parts is represented by the Aristotelian corpus, where Kepler could find humanistic and naturalistic philosophies combined into something that was supposed to surpass even the Bible itself.

Therefore, while portraying himself as a good Christian, Johannes Kepler was delving in secret, occult knowledge. As a result, he came up with theories and ideas that contradicted the Word of God and posed as being the only truth.

Apostle Paul in 1st Corinthians, 3, warned us of this danger, hundreds of years before Kepler, of how men would try to lie and to deceive us, claiming to know the ultimate truth and wisdom.

"For the wisdom of the world is foolishness with God. For it is written, "He catches the wise in their own craftiness."

The same apostle Paul warned us that, in the end, Satan himself will disguise himself as an angel of light and that he will prey on the weakest of souls, those souls who have turned their faces away from God and decided to trust the human tongue and its endless lies.

With all the warnings at hand, the people involved with science at that time, regardless in what area, accepted the Book of Nature without too much debate. It looked like someone had somehow managed to convince the great majority that scripture was no longer acceptable, therefore they needed something else, and The Book of Nature proved to be the perfect replacement.

Kepler Stated: "The Diversity of the phenomena of nature is so great, and the treasures are hidden in the heavens so rich, precisely in order that the human mind shall never be lacking in fresh nourishment."

His statement clearly defies the teaching of scripture, as he covertly tries to suggest that we have been wrong all along. Instead of God sitting over the heavens, now we have something completely different: no firmament, no windows of heaven, or waters above the firmament; they're all gone now.

What started as a weak attempt at complementing the Bible in its attempt to explain the natural world, thus it could not be in contradiction with the Bible, and yet, it became over the years a challenge at the authority of scripture and even replaced it eventually.

To me, this is an alarming precedent, the way in which a man-made concept or doctrine, call it what you will, took precedent over the Word of God. Kepler, and those like him, considered themselves as the priests of the Book of Nature, the servants of the Highest God:

"Since we astronomers are the priests of the Highest God in regard to the book of nature, it befits us to be thoughtful, not of the glory of our minds, but rather, above all else, of the glory of God."

Who was this god of theirs, I wonder, and what did they understand through that glory they speak of in such high regards? Maybe he thought that he was given access to a higher degree of understanding of the natural world and the heavens. He probably believed that he had a clearer path to the truth than the scriptures themselves offered and this is pure blasphemy.

In any case, his actions proved that he was convinced that scripture was not the ultimate measure of truth when it came to matters of the heavens or the natural world.

His so-called revelations convinced him that the heavens themselves had authority over the scripture and he needed nothing else to understand the complexity of what he was witnessing. Kepler embraced and preached this new doctrine to bring about a revolution in the field of astronomy, to change the laws and truths, so he could serve a different purpose.

Kepler was fully aware of the origins of the Book of Nature, and the involvement of ancient authorities (thousands of years old ideas/doctrines) and knew that his new doctrine was aligned with Pythagoras' philosophy.

Despite all 'legends' and perceptions, I believe that Kepler was, in fact, a very dangerous man, a man with a hidden agenda, who was determined to change our reality and our perception of the truth, and for that reason, he came disguised as an angel of light, a brilliant scientist and innovator, who simply wanted to take us out of the darkness and show us the truth.

Appearances can always be deceiving, especially when so much 'proof' is put in front of our eyes, and under the 'sacred' authority of science, even the worst enemies of humanity can pose as peaceful benefactors. Trust me when I tell you that they love to play with us and mess with our minds to take us away from our creator.

The adepts of the heliocentric theory came up with truths that needed to be believed, hundreds of years before we could even fly through the air, let alone fly into space. Now, let me ask you this, if they could not prove anything in fact, why did they push on with their ideas, struggling to convert everyone else to this new religion called Scientism? The answer is simple: they were on a hunt for veneration. They wanted to be regarded as gods themselves, since no one else knew what they knew, and they alone managed to dethrone God from the heavens in people's minds.

I often wonder if they think us to be ignorant and stupid enough to gobble down whatever we are fed, because the more I analyze the evolution of our space flight, the more I see how things became senseless and illogical.

Is it possible that they started to be afraid? I mean, we see the rockets going up, but only up to a point, and then they disappear. Maybe they hit on something hard and blew apart. Maybe they're sick of spending so much money to keep us asleep, and now, once they concocted new tools and ways, they decided to give up the idea of flying outside earth's orbit.

So many questions, with so many possible answers, but I know one thing for sure. Scientism will always have a replacement. These people who see themselves as gods will never leave an empty space, because they fear we will finally manage to see the truth. Therefore, they'll trade one lie for another, so they can keep us in this constant state of slumber and confusion.

It's time for us to wake up and realize that the Bible tells the only truth about the heavens, and God is the one residing above all of us, guarding and observing us, like an all-knowing and loving father.

You cannot fly outside the earth to land on something that is under the firmament. It makes no sense, and it would be obvious for most of us if we chose not to believe the Scientism lies, this fake science that keeps feeding us lies and deceptions one after another, poisoning our heads and hearts so we're no longer close to our creator, but rather willing to sell our souls to made up theories, invented by the power behind the wicked men who want to control the world in rebellion to God.

Scriptural evidence against the modern-day cosmology of the earth travelling around the sun is apparent in many verses in the Bible, but I will just touch on a few in this chapter.

The mobility of the sun

The most important biblical quote supporting a geocentric universe can be found in the Book of Joshua. This will be used as the starting point for our scriptural cosmology.

*Then spoke Joshua to the Lord in the day when the Lord gave the Amorites over to the men of Israel; and he said in the sight of Israel, "**Sun, stand thou still** at Gibeon, and thou Moon in the valley of Aijalon." **And the sun stood still**, and the moon stayed, until the nation took vengeance on their enemies. Is this not written in the Book of Jashar? **The sun stayed in the midst of heaven**, and did not hasten to go down for about a whole day. Joshua 10:12-13*

The miracle of Joshua appears again as a reference in The Book of Habakkuk.

The sun and moon stood still *in their habitation at the light of thine arrows as they sped, at the flash of thy glittering spear. Habakkuk 3:11*

The evidence in support of a geocentric model is overwhelming here. Joshua commanded the *sun* to stand still. He did not order the earth to cease rotating nor did he qualify his statement with the divine knowledge that the sun was merely made to *appear* stationary. The sun was commanded to stand still, because it is the sun that moves.

The stability of the earth

On the other side of the geocentric coin, if the sun moves, then the earth must not move. There are a few passages which more or less forbid the motion of the earth.

*Tremble before him, all earth; yea, **the world stands firm, never to be moved.***

1 Chronicles 16:30

*The Lord reigns; he is robbed in majesty; the lord is robbed, he is girded with strength. Yea, **the world is established; it shall never be moved**. Psalms93:1*

*Say among the nations, "The Lord reigns! Yea, **the world is established, it shall never be moved**; he will judge the peoples with equity." Psalms96:10*

Some will disregard the Bible as proof of anything with regards to the heliocentric versus geocentric debate but let me tell you that every experiment ever designed to detect the motion of the earth has failed to detect earth's motion and/or distinguish it from relative counter motion of the heavens. Many observations tell us that we are stationary, but science applies unproven assumptions to make us believe something else.

One experiment of importance in history was the The Michelson-Morley experiment. The Michelson–Morley experiment was a scientific experiment to find the presence and properties of a substance called aether, a substance believed to fill empty space. Michelson and Morley created this experiment to try and prove the theory that aether existed. They did this with a device called an interferometer.

It was reasoned that, if the speed of light were constant with respect to the proposed aether through which the Earth was moving, that motion could be detected by comparing the speed of light in the direction of the Earth's motion and the speed of light at right angles to the Earth's motion. No difference was found. This null result seriously discredited the aether theories and ultimately led to scientism embracing Albert Einstein's theory of relativity and moving further away from true science and embracing more of the theories that would discredit the Bible, while holding on to their Big Bang heliocentric universe.

Here is a list of experiments attempting to prove the rotation or movement of the Earth throughout history:

Sir George Biddel Airy...1871... failed.

Michelson-Morley...1887... failed.

Trouton-Noble...1901-1903... failed.

Nordmeyer-Bucherer...1903... failed.

Michelson-Gale-Pearson...1925... failed.

Rudolf Tomaschek...1925-1926... failed.

Chase...1926-1927... failed.

Hayden...1994... failed.

The Sagnac Effect..1913... failed.

Albert Einstein...theory of relativity.... failed.

EVERY SINGLE EXPERIMENT TO PROVE THE MOVEMENT OF THE EARTH HAS FAILED.

Chapter 7: Scientism and Space

For thou hast said in thine heart, I will ascend into heaven, I will exalt my throne above the stars of God: I will sit also upon the mount of the congregation, in the sides of the north: Isaiah 14:13

If we look back in history, we can see how the separation between science and occultism is a fairly modern thing. Back then, science or alchemy was strictly in bond with ancient knowledge and doctrines.

John Whiteside "Jack" Parsons

An interesting character at the beginning of the 20th century was John Whiteside Parsons, born in 1914, who was a boy with a passion for rockets. From a young age, he played and experimented with small rockets in the backyard of his parent's house with the help of his grandfather. Eventually, he became a rocket propulsion expert, a chemist and, above all, he got involved with Thelema, Alistair Crowley's new religion.

Parsons was also one of the initial founders of the JPL (Jet Propulsion Laboratory) and the one who created the first rocket engine to use a castable, composite rocket propellant. In fact, he was one of the pioneers of rocketry, in a time when rockets and magic were not so far apart from one another, judging by how outlandish rocket flying was considered back then. We could barely fly using propeller planes on low speeds, let alone control rockets that could fly a few times above the speed of sound. Yet Parsons did not give up on his dream and continued to research and develop his rockets further.

The interesting fact is that Parsons did not actually go to university and learned everything by himself thought experimenting. Therefore, what started as child's play with cardboard tubes, ended with building various rocket engines, fueled by various propellants. It's safe to say that Parson took the rocket from the field of science fiction and restored it to its rightful place, by creating a proper science for his childhood passion.

Soon, the government became interested in Parsons' developments, and even if he was regarded as an eccentric character due to his occult involvements during his private time, they went on with it, thus creating something certain people would call a monster (A big corporate, military, industrial concern).

When Parsons' development as a scientist and occultist reached a certain critical point, the people who were in fact behind his projects, and those throwing their money into this field, decided that his time was over. So, with a swift move, they removed his name and legacy from the rocketry history of the United States, wiping so clean behind him that people hardly know who John Whiteside Parsons really was.

If you are willing to try testing this idea, just pick one of the standard textbooks on rocketry and you will hardly find his name mentioned once or twice or not at all.

World War II goes by and we find ourselves in a Space Race. It was, in fact, a supremacy fight between capitalism and communism, two opposite ideologies that were fighting on the same front: they both saw God as obsolete and were trying to replace him with something else.

This sort of fierce battle, trying to prove the same thing, makes you wonder if, in fact, we're talking about the same people playing on both sides at the same time with only one purpose in mind: to fool the masses and keep the people caught up in this sick game of theirs. This is a vast subject we could elaborate on some other time.

For now, let us get back to our Scientism and Space dispute and the occultism behind it.

As I mentioned already, in the 1960s and 1970s, came the Era of Moon landings, where every year or two, we staged another landing and then another one. After a while, it started feeling like a moon flight was something like a bus ride and that we could do one whenever we felt like it.

Now, I want you to pay attention to this character: Werner Von Braun. A Brilliant scientist as the textbooks depict him, but at the same time, a man with a complicated history. Initially, he was a Nazi scientist under Hitler's direct supervision and had one goal: to create the perfect weapon, an intercontinental ballistic missile, capable of hitting targets thousands of miles away, killing hundreds or thousands of people, depending on the warhead.

Von Braun was an important character in the Nazi structures. He was part of the propaganda and part of the Nazi occultism. He was deeply rooted in their occult teachings and proceedings, and it is safe to say that he came with all that baggage after the war ended and the US soldiers scooped him out of Germany through the operation Paper Clip.

His record was suddenly cleaned and from a war criminal, Von Braun was turned into a respectable citizen of the United States, put in charge of the national space program.

The treachery is obvious! No one in their right minds would place a project that's so strategic into the hands of a foreigner, and the fact they supposedly did it, show us the lie behind the whole Apollo program. At first, they lied about Von Braun's past, saying that he was forced to build those V1 and V2 rockets. They said he had no other choice, but I don't really buy those words. Von Braun could have just said 'no' and faced the consequences.

It looks to me that it's easier to blame someone else for the horror and destruction that you cause. I guess it helps you sleep better at night and that's in case Von Braun and his peers had any humanity and decency left in them. Because he did not come alone, but he brought his whole team to the US, which was made up of many people.

Once this agenda was put in place, they began brainwashing our children, introducing them into this space-world, with toys such as G.I Joe, the famous astronaut all sixties children will gladly remember. The children did not know whether space flight was actually achievable, they did not know the facts or the numbers, but it did not matter that much. If they could embed in their mind that it was possible to fly up there, into space, that is where it was going to stay for eternity.

Their move was clever indeed, because they targeted the most vulnerable area of our society: the children. If an adult can be able to think critically and analyze the information he receives, a child will only look up to authority, and in this case, the television was a strong authority. Even today, people live with the impression that it can't be possible for those running the TV station to sell lies to the masses. It is widely believed that the state, through its institutions, is controlling the mass media, so it only presents verified information, therefore the truth.

Unfortunately, the TV has only been a tool for propaganda, and back in the day, it enjoyed an even greater level of truth from the people, since there were no alternative means of information (such as the internet today).

As a result, children were brainwashed into believing the space crap from an early age, so later in life, they would not doubt or question this idea.

An interesting event took place during the Apollo 11 press conference, where journalists noticed that all three of the astronauts looked as if something were seriously wrong. I mean, if you completed the greatest achievement in mankind's history, you would be so happy, yet they looked very despondent and deeply troubled, as if they were perpetrating the greatest lie on the world.

Armstrong, Aldrin, and Collins at Apollo 11 Press Conference

Anyway, I guess, over the years, that this episode during the press conference was forgotten by the world and all that was left in people's memories was the remarkable achievement of our astronauts. Using basic technology, no experience at all, and having the most rudimentary tools, they crossed space and landed on the moon, and then came back to tell the tale. It sounds a little farfetched to me, but then, who am I to question all this, right?

We all saw President Obama talking about space and what we should do next, and when some people suggested we should go back to the moon and end the dispute once and for all, he blatantly smiled and said, "We've been there already!"

I laughed when watching that video, because I could not help myself. Obama tried to make it look like we had mapped and explored every single inch of the moon and there is absolutely nothing else for us to see there anymore. For the sake of the argument, let's say that we landed on the moon. How much did we get to explore? A few yards? Grabbed a couple of rocks and then we came back? Is that all we can do on the Moon?

Now, let me rephrase a little bit. Is that all we should do? I mean, judging by their words, the Moon is incredible, and we should go back right now and start exploring every inch of it until we can safely say that we've done everything possible and now it's time to move on... to Mars or further planets in the universe.

But what if we're not doing it, because it is impossible to do it, huh? What if the moon is not actually where they say it is and we can't land on it as if it were some terra firma waiting for us?

Well, I say the lie should end right here, right now! We know they have been lying to us for hundreds of years about the millions and billions of years of ancient history. They've been lying to us about the evolution of species and how we supposedly evolved from speechless monkeys. They lied to us about the solar system, the universe, the stars, the moon, the sun... You name it. The list can go on and on and that's because Satan's lies are endless.

The devil works in ways we rarely understand. His means are wicked and these people who have associated themselves with him, borrowed those means and clever lies, they know how to trick a man's mind perfectly, how to manipulate whole populations to serve their purposes.

And the worst part for us is that their lies will never stop! We're being lied to about our identity, God's identity, and our purpose on this Earth.

Satan's greatest weakness is represented by the fact that he cannot create life the way God does, as this is God's exclusive prerogative, therefore his only chance is to corrupt God's creation. Through his tricks and manipulation, Satan undergoes a relentless battle over our souls and tries constantly to draw us to his side, in one way or another. His final goal is to transform God's creation, people made in the image of God into carnal creatures of darkness, where the soul is tainted by sin and corruption and lies.

As the Space Age reached its peak and people became more and more involved with the new 'discoveries', such as new types of stars, solar systems, and planets, the lie became more complex and more overwhelming. It looked like we were throwing ourselves into a realm we did not know and had never seen with our own eyes or in our lifetimes, and yet, the 'scientists' never stopped making assumptions. It looked like everything in the universe was greater, bigger, and more complex than what we have, therefore we needed to bow our heads with humility and reconsider our place in the cosmos.

Our sun was nothing but a medium yellow star, somewhere at the edge of a regular galaxy, and we were living on a rather small planet compared to what's out there. I mean, compared to our own solar system, we are situated somewhere in between, but on a large scale, we were nothing but talking ants. Isn't this convenient? God's ultimate creation rendered to the level of bugs! Yes, they want us to think of ourselves as bugs, who deserve nothing but to be squashed whenever they say so.

God says how he created the moon, the sun, and the stars on the fourth day, and how, at that moment, the earth had already been created. The Bible clearly instructs us on how we were in the center of God's creation, his masterpiece, but they keep insisting that, on the contrary, we were nothing but an accident of a random collision of rocks.

When looking at Genesis, we understand the logic and the order with which God created the world. Now, let me ask you this: After creating the earth, there was no sun or moon, around what was the earth spinning? It was spinning like a lunatic around empty space the way they are trying to convince us, or maybe the sun was already there, but did not have its switch turned on, so nobody could see it.

It's hard for me to see through the Scientism gibberish, because it makes no sense, and every time someone comes out with a piece of proof that contradicts their theory, they turn around, wrap the old idea into a new casing, smile at you and say: "Well, you did not really understand what we were trying to say; here's how things are."

Quite laughable how Scientism is trying to distort the facts that are written right there in the first pages of the Bible. You don't have to shuffle too much to find the truth, because it's right there at the beginning of the Bible. And if you still have doubts about the truths written in the Bible, all you need to do is go outside your home and look at the world with your own eyes. Observe the nature, the reality surrounding you carefully, and you will certainly reach the same conclusions as the Bible did thousands of years ago.

The truth is simple and let me tell you why. Regardless of the technology we have right now and all the awesome gadgets that make our life easier, we're basically the same as a man and woman who lived on this Earth 5 thousand years ago. Our hearts beat the same, our eyes see the same, and our minds work in the same manner. For that reason, if we choose to look at the world, we'll see the same things, the same wonders and miracles that God put there.

It's not really that hard to see the truth, if you choose to look. Unfortunately, our eyes have been turned away from the truth with all kinds of dazzling effects and man-made distractions, so that we're not able to spot the truth anymore. Among all this confusion and cheap entertainment, it looks like we have lost our touch. We lost that sixth sense that makes our direct connection with God possible. As a final piece, Satan and his minions are trying to make us forget God completely. They're trying to turn Him and His creation into a fat joke worthy of being laughed at, even by small children.

Once this is achieved, he knows we're going to be lost forever. Fortunately for us, we have not reached that point in time yet and still have time to turn things around in our favor. We still have enough time at our disposal to realize and understand who our true Creator and Father is and to return to His arms.

Chapter 8: Scientism and NASA

Ye are blessed of the LORD which made heaven and earth. The heaven, even the heavens, are the LORD'S but the earth hath he given to the children of men. Psalm 115:16-17

After we managed to conquer the seas and the skies, mankind started looking up and wanted to see and explore what was beyond the Earth. It looked like we had reached a point in our development where we could actually achieve such a thing.

With the discovery of the airplane in the early 20th century, and then, with the invention of the rocket, they were set to 'provide' us with another truth about the heavens.

With the Cold war between the USSR and the United States, another war began, and that was the war over space and who could get there sooner. After the Russians sent Sputnik, the first man-made satellite in orbit on October 4th, 1957, then the first Dog in orbit (Laika), culminating with Yuri Gagarin, as the first man in space, the United States felt left behind in this war. It was clear that they needed to step up the game, if they did not want to remain in second place in history.

For that reason, President Dwight D. Eisenhower signed the National Aeronautics and Space Act in 1958, creating NASA, as a rather civilian-oriented agency, with the scope of developing applications in space science and exploration.

Original NASA logo

Once NASA was established, it was clear that, in just a few short years, great achievements needed to be accomplished, so the US recovered the lost terrain against the USSR. As expected, soon after that, President John F. Kennedy announced the next target of the United States with a daring and fiery speech.

The US was going to put the first man on the Moon, an achievement that would overshadow everything the Russians had achieved up to that point. Now, keep in mind that this entire story that was surfacing between the two super powers was nothing but a big show to further convince us of one of the biggest deceptions in history.

What started as a tool of destruction (Von Braun's V1 and V2 rockets) was converted later, after the end of World War II, into a tool of science and space exploration. Once the Saturn rockets were built, it looked like we were finally on the brink of conquering the heavens.

This was going to be a moment of truth and the whole of humankind held its breath, because we were finally going to see if Copernicus, Kepler, and all those 'brilliant' astronomers were actually right. To Scientism, space flight was going to be the final frontier and the final proof that would convince humanity that God is not up there and that science was correct with the Big Bang heliocentric universe they had managed to sell us for over 500 years.

So, with a final effort, towards the end of the 1950's and the beginning of the 1960's, man was finally catapulted into space. Quite convenient, isn't it? After the biggest war that had people traumatized and confused from so much death and destruction, the final proof came onto the stage.

As the leaders of the day said with pompous words: it was time for a new world order, a new philosophy of life, and a new set of moral truths. Indeed, it was, and what better solution for mankind than changing their religious paradigm for good? The heavens were exactly as they said, and they could prove it now!

"We choose to go to the Moon" by President John F. Kennedy

Following the 'space battle' between America and the Russians, the next logical step was represented by the moon. There was a great fuss around this subject and President Kennedy's fiery speeches managed to excite the crowds. People were cheering and clapping their hands for something they thought they knew, but did they know anything at all?

Even now, I don't believe we ever managed to set foot on the moon, and in order to prove my point to you, I will give you a few more details. Let's say the moon is right there, where they say it is, 240,000 miles (384,400 km away from Earth), and we could step on it, if we had the technology. Back in the day, we barely had computers, and the computational power was next to nothing, and yet they keep throwing at us the fact that it was more than necessary. Those old computers can't even compare with the phone you're carrying in your pocket right now, and yet we allegedly went to the moon, only when we had crappy computers. After things started to develop and evolve, we stopped doing it 'for some reason'.

No one knows for certain why we have stopped going to the moon, but I am telling you we did not stop at all, because we did not get there at all. Everything people saw on their screens back home was nothing, but a smoke and mirrors show, created with a precise purpose: to convince people that there was no shred of doubt that

88

we're living in a heliocentric universe where everything revolves around everything at terrible speeds.

Another contradiction that appears to make no sense for any person who chooses to judge things with their own minds, are the pictures taken by Neil Armstrong and his fellow astronauts of the Apollo program. The supposed pictures of Earth are of a horrendous quality. It looks like we had computing capacities to takes us to the moon and back, but we could not get our hands on a decent camera. The resolution of those pictures is absolutely disappointing, not to mention, when you actually look into the pictures, you will find many problems, which will be discussed in a future chapter.

Anyway, in order for things to fit perfectly in the Copernican paradigm, all the conclusions that were drawn after these 'Moon and Space' expeditions said only one thing: The Earth is spinning and revolving around the sun.

With all the gaps and inconsistencies, with all the unexplained facts and impossible outcomes, humanity was presented with another universal truth: We were the gods now. We conquered all the dimensions of our existence. With us ends everything.

Looking back in history, right when those events were unfolding, we can see people with tears in their eyes, so happy and proud that we had reached the Moon, that it looks like nothing else really matters in this life. God, our sins, and responsibilities, our duty to this life, were all absent now, because we reached the heavens before we died. Our old dream, that started with Daedalus and Icarus, was finally accomplished, when we reached the place reserved only for the gods.

With the Space Age, we began living a delusion, where we imagined we would soon conquer the rest of the 'solar system' and in just a few short years, we would be masters of the universe. So great was the deception and so well built, that people started believing genuinely that we could do such a thing. Now that the heliocentric paradigm was well embedded in our heads, it was time for a new chapter in our lie.

That's how a lie works. To keep people trapped inside it, you need to keep the lie alive, therefore you need to feed it from time to time, otherwise, people will start doubting their reality, and gradually, the lie would fade away, exposing the truth.

The heavens were ours now! Great promises were made by scientists and other men of power, like presidents and other influential people, and we were sold a fantasy to feed our ever-expanding ego, the same ego that the scientists helped create in the first place, with their theories and auto-imposed truths.

Another aspect that needs to be taken into consideration is the Van Allen radiation belt, that supposedly surrounds earth, and it would kill any living thing that tries to leave the low earth orbit. The entire scientific world agrees with this theory, and yet, when it is brought into discussion regarding the moon missions, all we can get is a faint smile in the corner of their mouths. A gesture that is supposed to place the rest of us in offside, because they know better and we should not ask so many questions anyway. We're not scientists, but mere mortals, who should think less and listen to what they have to say more.

You see, this is yet another unsolved mystery regarding our flight into the heavens and beyond low earth orbit, if there is such a thing anyway. The lack of logic and debate surprises me even today, as some of the astronauts who were part of the Apollo program and who are still alive, refuse to answer verifying questions.

To me, it looks like they don't have all the answers, despite the fact that they say they stepped on the moon's surface. It makes me wonder sometimes what it would take to make man live his entire life inside a lie. Would it be money? A comfortable life? I could not tell for sure, because there comes a time in a man's life, when neither money, fame, nor glory make any sense. The only answer I could come up with was that maybe they are recruited for their qualities, even before they put a 'filming' suit on. I am sure we'll find the truth sooner or later.

For some reason though, the 'Moon Odyssey' as I like to call it, ended abruptly; even faster than it came into being. So, on December 11[th,] 1972, our last 'moon rocket' took off, and we never set foot on the moon again. Despite the fact that computers boomed, and the internet was born, we did not even consider putting a man on the moon or sending astronauts beyond low earth orbit ever again.

Right now, as I write these words, I have in mind one of NASA's astronauts, Terry Virts, who stated that all we can do now is fly in low earth orbit, but we are currently developing some new technology that will allow us to go much further. Strange, isn't it? After almost 50 years, we can only get to low earth orbit, but back then, we were clearly more advanced and could reach the moon!

Something does not add up in their theories and declarations, because right now, computers are clearly more intelligent, and we even have a sort of incipient A.I (artificial intelligence), and yet, we just can't go anywhere. Why is it that, back then, flying to the moon seemed like a piece of cake, therefore we did it several times, and now, we just look at it from a distance? As a matter of fact, all we're doing right now is looking at things from a distance and making an assumption based on what we think we saw.

Isn't it amazing how we regressed over the years? I mean, Darwin kept saying that species evolved, they improve themselves to increase their chances of survival. That should be the theory, but in practice, we only made steps backward from the 60s and 70s, until this present day. It looks like we are afraid of going out there, as if there is some boogeyman, waiting to eat us if we dare to cross the boundary. It's either that or we just can't do it (and I'm not saying 'anymore'), because if we could do it once, with that basic technology, I am sure we could do it now, no problems! What I am trying to underline here is that we never actually reached the moon, let alone stepped onto its surface.

Right now, we look with humbleness at the moon and the other celestial bodies in our solar system and hope that, one day, we have the technology to visit and explore them. How is this? Half a century ago, we were bursting with boldness and confidence and it looked like the whole universe was ours, and now we turn around with our tail between our legs. This whole situation should make anyone really question NASA and the entire space paradigm which we've been taught.

If you're a little bit older, you'll remember all the Star Trek and Star Wars movies. We basically grew up watching those movies and we were excited to see how humanity was exploring the universe and meeting so many new and interesting species. That was indeed just science- fiction, but we all hoped that, soon, the fiction will be taken out of the equation and we'd have pure science and actual exploration of the galaxy, at least.

This explosion of space exploration movies was due to the social trend of that time and the great promises we were hearing from NASA almost every day. With the involvement of Hollywood, people started believing space exploration was, in fact, possible and the myriad of planets and new solar system sparked their imagination.

Too bad it was nothing but a big, fat lie, an optical illusion created to keep people with their eyes stuck to the screens. The films were very realistic, and you would say that people reached those distant planets. This makes me wonder if NASA did not use the same technology to fake the moon landing and make people believe in a false thing. After all, to them, it did not really matter if they landed on the moon or not, what really mattered was people's perception of this subject and if the effects were indeed worthy enough to be deemed as reality.

At the end of the day, Science-Fiction remained just that, while real science made a step back into the shadows, leaving room for doubt and interpretation. In our minds as space fans, NASA was nothing but the precursor to Star Fleet and the Federation of Planets, where Earth played a leading role. Imagine the disappointment, when we realized NASA was never achieving such a thing, but was instead a huge, money-eating machine, that did not accomplish anything significant at all.

The internet is full of articles and videos, where people debunk every single aspect of the lunar missions. And I am not talking about regular people, who discuss over a beer or glass of wine. I am talking about true professionals, scientists, and engineers, who have the tools and the knowledge to prove that we never actually landed on the moon and that the whole thing was filmed here on earth, in a desert, with the help of cables and strings, to give the impression of low gravity.

Back then though, people did not actually question the Moon landing or anything else that people from NASA were saying. We were too dazzled and mesmerized by the idea, that we gobbled down everything and decided to trust every word they said. After all, in the United States, we were part of NASA, in a way, since it was a government agency, therefore, we felt like it was carrying our pride to the moon, too.

Pride, one of the greatest sins of mankind, stood again in the way and prevented us from seeing the truth. We really wanted to believe that we were capable of such a thing and we chose to convince ourselves that we were the best, since we achieved it.

I was a part of that huge mass of believers too, but eventually, I decided to look again and analyze the facts. I decided to look into it myself, with different eyes. No preconceptions, no pride, or pre-established truths, just facts and a clear mind... and boy, did I discover the lies.

There are a lot of problems with these missions, things that make no sense, but the thing that kept popping up in my head were those astronaut suits that Neil Armstrong and his fellow astronauts wore during their missions. I mean, those things don't look like they could protect you from a mild breeze while walking on the beach, let alone keep you safe from the enormous amounts of radiation falling onto your shoulders, if you'd been right in the middle of the Earth and the Moon.

The costumes look like they are made up of simple cotton. There was no complicated technology attached to them (of course, because there wasn't any at that time), no sight of safety measures, or anything else. I am surprised that NASA could not come up with something more intriguing, more eye-catching, just for the sake of the show. But anyway, let us focus on other aspects of the mission, such as the Van Allen radiation belt. We talked about it a bit previously, thus we know that extreme levels of radiation will kill anything alive in less than a day, and yet, our astronauts managed to pass through it in jumpsuits and tin hats, a couple of times back and forth, and not one astronaut was ever affected.

A funny thought comes to my mind now about the radiation belt. They say that what you don't know can't hurt you. I guess the astronauts did not know about the Van Allen Belt then, and that's why they managed to get back safe and sound. It looks like the scientists from NASA failed to tell them that they might die a gruesome death, as soon as they left low earth orbit, therefore, they were just fine.

Leaving the jokes aside, it really makes no sense how conditions existent at the time of the Apollo Missions did not prevent us from getting to the moon, but now they do. Another aspect that would raise suspicions with every logical person, is the fact that NASA lost all the telemetry data and destroyed the technology that allowed us to travel to the moon. It is unacceptable how these so-called scientists from NASA laugh in our face, when they tell us that they just can't find the data! What? Who took it? I am sure someone must be responsible, if that data was there in the first place. We live in a democracy with checks and balances, therefore, there must be an institution capable enough to get to the bottom of things… or not?

If this deception had its roots at the highest levels, it clear to me that powerful men clearly want to keep us in the dark, even today in the age of information, and it looks like they are doing a great job, too!

Don Pettit, who is a NASA astronaut at this moment, stated that he would "Go to the moon in a nanosecond, the problem is that we don't have the technology to do that anymore. We used to, but we destroyed all that technology, and it's a painful process to build it back again."

I ended this quote with a troubling question on my mind. I mean, the man says it clearly, that we can't fly to the moon anymore, because we don't have the technology… anymore! It seems that we used to have it, but we don't have it now. Doesn't this ring a bell to you? The man says this, with a straight face, as if there's nothing wrong with his statement. It's unbelievable how these people can look at us and say these words, knowing they are spending billions of your tax payer dollars each year. The fact that this agency gets 52 million dollars a day makes me sick.

Leaving the money aside, I think there is another pressing matter we need to analyze and that's the fact that we allegedly 'destroyed' the technology that would allow us to get to the Moon and back.

Why would we destroy such a wonderful technology in the first place? What government in its right mind would destroy something that cost billions to build in the first place? Maybe they did it because they knew it was fake and all they wanted was to cover their tracks?

To me, this is the most plausible explanation. Besides, we have the footage, for better or worse, and I guess the people behind this scheme decided it was all we needed. To them, it was clear that at some point, some curious people would come in and start digging for the truth and that was not something they were going to let happen, therefore, they erased all the traces from the face of the earth.

Another frightening aspect that made me shiver was the fact that people who were directly involved in the Apollo program, people such as Gene Kranz, who was a flight director for Apollo 11, claim they have no idea where the telemetry of that mission is. He admits he has no idea if the data is even in existence and even if we were able to find it, we don't have the machines to play it back.

REALLY? We can't find some old computer or another way to read the data? I mean, we can tell that some bone of a supposed dinosaur is 40 million years old, but we can't read some tapes that are only 40-50 years old? It looks like no matter how much we try to get some answers from these folks, all we're receiving are made up excuses and reasons as to why we should stop looking into it. We're not going to stop. That's a certainty.

Dr. David Williams, who is a NASA archivist, raises his hands in the air, while admitting he has no clue where the telemetry of the Apollo program ended up. He also says that he tried in vain to get to the bottom of it, but all his efforts did not lead him anywhere.

If you heard this for the first time in your life, I bet you'd think it's crazy, right? I mean, how come an agency so big and so well-funded can't find its own information? It's ludicrous and real at the same time, and the people from NASA are not even trying to hide it. Their attitude is self-sufficient when they say these things, as if they want us to read through the lines: so, what are you going to do now?

They know we don't have the technology and the means to go up there and prove they are wrong, but instead, we have common sense and the Bible, which is the ultimate truth and the Bible teaches us the Moon is closer than they say and those hundreds of thousands of miles are nothing but a made-up story.

When looking through their inconsistencies and lies, it's hard to believe NASA's story anymore, with all of their so called 'achievements'. They have all sorts of campaigns and press conferences and they post new things all the time, but they are nothing but CGI. When people asked NASA if the Earth picture is 100% real, they could not say this about any of their pictures.

NASA keeps telling us they are editing the pictures, because they're trying to make them more beautiful and that the 'real' ones aren't so impressive.

What a minute! I don't remember that we ever asked to be impressed, we wanted the truth. We wanted to see a real picture of the Earth and what do we get in return? Digitally mastered copies and overlaid pictures, so we don't even know what is there anymore. Also, when you do a search on the internet for "real pictures of earth from space", all you get is composites, renderings, paintings, cartoons, etc. Where are the real pictures, NASA?

I wonder, why aren't they showing us a single, unedited picture of Earth? Is there something we aren't supposed to see and for that reason, they keep brushing everything off and keep covering stuff? Also, fish-eye lensed pictures don't count.

Right now, we have photo cameras that can zoom impressively and from the surface of the earth, we can take decent photos of the moon. We can see the craters and the big formations (an aspect that would suggest the moon was not that far away from us). Now imagine what we could do with one of those super advanced cameras installed on satellites, how clearly, we would be able to see almost everything and every rock on the moon, and yet, the satellites are not turned in that direction. I for one would love to see a zoomed in picture of the earth, showing buildings and planes upside down. It should be very possible to do.

We supposedly have spying satellites that can see what brand your paper cup is, while you are having your morning coffee, but they can't see if the lunar module is still there. That thing is pretty big, I'd say, and easy to spot, and yet nobody cared to look.

Also, supposedly the Europeans, the Chinese, and the Russians, have satellites in orbit as well, but none of them dared to take a peek at the moon surface? New reports have claimed that the Chinese have sent satellites around the moon, thus the dark side of the moon argument does not work anymore, and yet, we still don't have a picture showing us the rover. "There it is… Stop doubting poor Armstrong and his giant leap!"

It would appear we're facing a global conspiracy. Scientism has spread to all corners of the earth and has taken over all the countries. This is a malady worse than the plague and it will not stop until it has 'infected' every single individual, regardless of his/her religion or creed.

Now regarding those satellites we keep talking about, we have no certainty that they are up there either, but for the sake of the argument, we discussed how unbelievable it is that we don't have a clear picture of the moon's surface. If I dared to ask for a picture of a satellite, I guess I would get the same answer, "NO". At least a real picture, because, right now, with Photoshop and all the 3D graphic designing, it would be quite impossible to tell fiction from reality. Even for a specialist, it would be difficult to tell the difference, let alone for regular folk, who have no knowledge.

Unfortunately for NASA, when they first staged the moon landings, the forgery means were not so developed, and we can clearly see their amateurism and their ridiculous attempts at CGI.

If you don't believe my words, just search for one of NASA's press conferences. The subject is unimportant, be it the Mars rover program or related to the space station, it's your pick, because you're going to see the same thing. A bunch or clueless people gathered behind a table, men and women who look like they have no idea what they are talking about. They look like they are lost and confused and have no idea why they are there in the first place. Plus, the answers they are giving to the reporters are something of a sixth-grade level.

It is unbelievable how people who are supposed to be the best professionals in the world look like they don't know a thing. Should this be the truth? Or maybe they are just embarrassed that they must lie to people upfront and try to keep it as low as possible. It's hard for me to tell what goes through those people's minds, but what can be seen on the exterior is really ridiculous.

These press conferences that are supposed to be episodes of revelation are turned into "Sorry, I can't tell you that!" Those people from NASA come in front of people and have the audacity to deny the answers. From what I recall, NASA was a government agency, so what's with all this secrecy? And besides, why are we throwing so much money at them, if they're not going to tell us what they found... in case they found anything?

So, you see, that's why people should start to walk away from NASA and stop believing every new discovery they announce weekly. Their attitude is one of the causes, because, if, at first, they looked like they were interested in explaining bits and pieces to the public, now they are not even struggling to look like they care about what people think.

NASA's actions are full of contradictions. They can't show us a clear picture of the moon, with all the gear we supposedly left there 50 years ago, and yet, just recently, they showed us stunning pictures of Pluto, a planet or whatever is called today, that's like 5 billion miles away from Earth. That is a heck of wi-fi signal NASA receives, considering the fact that they cannot tell us what format the pictures from Mars we're getting back are.

It looks to me like we'll never get a straight answer from NASA, as they will always try to lie and hide the truth from us. They show us only small bits that they deem acceptable for us to see, while they keep all the rest hidden from the world. I have stopped trusting these people a long time ago, because I understood that NASA is just another tool of Scientism, supposed to make us believe their lies. With made up pictures and a bunch of CGI effects, they think they can fool the whole world, but they are far from achieving their goal, now that the tables are turning.

Another aspect that made me wonder a little bit were the names chosen for their space missions: Mercury, Gemini, Apollo, and how these names were deeply rooted in the occult. I realized that NASA was a harmless public space agency only on the outside, because we can see the pagan idolatry behind the curtain, the same as with the secret societies that were basking in paganism and idolatry.

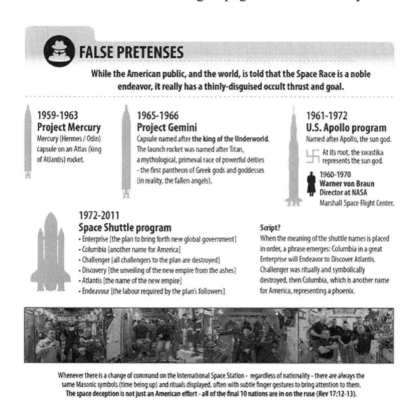

People might have thought those names were chosen because they sounded cool, but they carried a hidden meaning, a hidden agenda, and the people from NASA chose them so that they could draw a signal for those willing to comprehend. Their purpose was not to explore space, because they knew it was impossible, as there wasn't such a thing out there, but this did not stop them from cultivating old religions and beliefs that went back thousands of years.

Occultism is at the core of NASA and, judging from the people who were determinant for the agency (Jack Parsons, Alistair Crowley, L. Ron Hubbard) and others, who were the adepts of pagan theology, it easy to understand the efforts and struggle to disprove everything the Bible is teaching us. Their end goal is to show us a different 'truth' (fabricated or not), so they can take us away from God, the true Creator. For that reason, they're willing to lie and fabricate all sorts of 'proof', from new habitable planets, to distant stars, and maybe someday, an extraordinary external threat that is supposed to shake us in our boots, and maybe make us a little bit more docile and more willing to give up our freedom.

Chapter 9: Scientism and the Earth

I saw four angels standing on the four corners of the earth, holding the four winds of the earth, that the wind should not blow on the earth, nor the sea, nor on any tree: Revelation 7:1

In this chapter, we are going to talk about the earth. This magnificent place that God created for us to live in, to prosper, and to multiply. This Earth we call home and which, over the centuries, took different forms and meanings, depending on the current worldviews installed by the ruling classes.

Those malevolent people changed our perception of our beloved home, distorted its shape in our eyes, and eventually, they tried to turn it into something insignificant, mediocre, worthy of being trashed by our actions and wrong doings, but we have our true home, that's what you all need to keep in mind, regardless of how many 'super-earths' (whatever that might mean) they find each week, the real Earth is just one!

The battle between the dome and the globe

Now, turning back to the present day, just ask yourself, how many times have you seen the earth rendered as a globe, a perfect ball floating alone through the space? How many times have you seen this ball projection in your lifetime, then, in a year, then, in a single day?

From images you can find all over the web, in text books, to paintings, toys, commercials, and corporate logos, we are surrounded by this idea, as if the promoters behind it are trying to keep us locked, hypnotized always, even in our sleep. Our subconsciousness is under assault at all times, and from the earliest ages, we had this idea stuffed down our throats. We all remember the globe, carefully positioned in every class, even in kindergarten, when we couldn't care less about the shape of the earth, if we have toys to play with.

We did not know what was going on with us, but they knew clearly that the sooner they got us under their 'globe spell', the harder it would be for us to break free and realize the lie standing right in front of our eyes.

I can see how our collective subconsciousness is trapped and bombarded with this illusion from a plethora of angles. From advertising, to art, news, and entertainment, the globe projection is so deeply and thoroughly implanted in our minds, that it reached a point where it became the epitome of the unquestionable. So deeply rooted the globe has become in our minds that most people laugh when presented with an alternative. This so-called universal truth managed to blind people from the truth, so much so that most of them aren't willing to listen to the arguments anymore, regardless of how solid those arguments might be.

This public perception was most certainly strengthened by public figures, such as news anchors, politicians, and famous people in general (Obama, the perfect example), who mocked the 'flat earthers' and their conspiracies.

Right now, if you dare to speak against the dogma, when the shape of the earth is in discussion, you're quickly discredited, called different names (conspiracy kook, conspiracy buff, you name it!). The word 'conspiracy' itself has gotten a laughable meaning, where the concern has moved from those responsible of the conspiracy to those calling upon it. Isn't this so convenient for those who want to conceal the truth from the rest of the world? To convince the masses to laugh at someone who wants to unveil the truth, instead of opening their eyes and listening? I am sure this is so much easier for Scientism, after so many years and efforts on their side, people have turned on each other now. Quite brilliant.

This whole masquerade has been possible, unfortunately, because of the human ego and hubris. Most of the time, our pride prevents us from seeing the actual truth and we have an incredible power to convince ourselves that something isn't there, even if it is. Our mind just does not work, if we choose for it not to… And we can have all the proof and evidence in the world, but it would still be worthless, as our eyes will remain closed.

Our chapters are interlinked, because all we have talked about so far, and all that's about to follow, have something in common. All these ideas are part of the same scheme and can't work one without each other. The promoters of Scientism knew they had to create a gigantic lie to confuse people and prevent them from getting to the bottom of things.

The earth issue and the globe theory are a parts of the bigger whole, called the Big Bang cosmology. Without the Big Bang and the ever-expanding universe, we cannot have a globe, simply because we just could not explain this phenomenon.

In Isaiah 40:21-22, we find the following:

"Have ye not known? Have ye not heard? Hath it not been told you from the beginning? Have yet not understood from the foundations of the earth? It is that sitteth upon the CIRCLE OF THE EARTH, and the inhabitants thereof are as grasshoppers; that stretcheth out the heavens as a curtain, and spreadeth them out as a tent to dwell in…"

Also "The heaven is my throne and the earth is my footstool." Isaiah 66:1

"…the earth, for it is his footstool…" Mathew 5:35

These are only a few excerpts from the Bible that underline clearly Earth's shape and purpose. As God created it for us to be under his guidance and supervision, and since it is His footstool, we understand how the firmament is over the Earth. Indeed, it has a solidity to it, the whole construct being propped up like a tent, for us to dwell in.

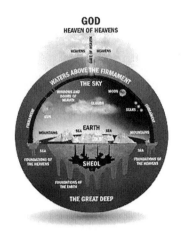

Hebrew cosmology pictures the Earth as a flat construct, situated somewhere in between the underworld (Sheol) and the upper world (the heavens), and ultimately the heavens of heavens, where God resided. The ground, the waters, and everything else residing on Earth were depicted as stationary, while everything else moved (the moon, the sun, the stars, and the wandering stars). The earth was seen as the center of the universe, God's most majestic creation, therefore, it could not move, as God did not move from the heavens.

Earth included all the other 'cosmic elements' previously mentioned, and as a whole, it was standing on great pillars.

"...the pillars of the earth are LORD'S, and he hath set the world upon them." –II Samuel 2:8

"Which shaketh the earth out of her place, and the pillars thereof tremble." Job 9:6

"... the foundations of the world were discovered, at the rebuking of the lord, at the blast of the breath of his nostrils." II Samuel 22:16 & Psalm 18:15

As you can see, the Bible is filled with details about the world's structure, and yet, Scientism insists on telling us that the Bible is wrong and that they have the actual truth.

Once, with the Copernican revolution and the introduction of the heliocentric model, little by little, the image of the flat earth was wiped from people's mind, to be replaced with a spinning ball, wandering aimlessly through space. Now that the earth was round and there were no heavens, the new dogma could easily exclude God from the equation as a creator and as a guardian of humanity.

Scientism could not stand Christianity and its connection with God, therefore, they started a revolution against God's creation and against God.

With all their efforts, Scientism could never disprove God and the Bible, and that's because they did not have the facts, only theories, and some flawed theories at that.

Now, let us return to the Bible, and study the structure of the Earth more in depth. In Genesis, it says that, at the beginning, it was just water and darkness, and God decided to separate the waters in order to create the earth. It might sound odd for those who choose not to believe, but God created a solid structure, The Firmament, to protect us from the water above.

"And God said, let there be a firmament in the midst of the waters, and let it divide waters from the waters. And God made the firmament and divided the waters which were under the firmament from the waters which were above the firmament: and it was so. And God called the firmament Heaven." Genesis 1:6-8

"Hast thou with him spread out the sky, which is strong and as a molten looking glass?" Job 37:18

We see here clearly how the firmament is not just a figure of speech, or something to be interpreted, but rather a solid structure, something concrete, made up of a transparent material, designed to protect us from any external threat.

God's throne is also depicted in the Bible and how it is situated right above the firmament.

"And above the firmament that was over their heads was the likeness of a throne, as the appearance of a sapphire stone: and upon the likeness of the throne was the likeness as the appearance of a man above upon it." Ezekiel 1:26

Now, let me ask you this: if, in the Bible, there are so many references to the actual structure of the earth and so many details are given, why would some people struggle so much to change the general perception? Would it be their oversized ego? Or some kind of hidden agenda? One thing is clear though, if some man manages to overthrow the Word of God, in the eyes of his peers he will be considered a god, and there's no greater proof of vanity in this world.

All emperors and dictators over the ages yearned to be praised as a god. From the oldest times (Egypt, Babylon, Rome), rulers struggled to convince people that they were sons of God or gods themselves. This vanity is not characteristic only to despots and emperors, but common men also, men who sought to challenge God and his creation, mocking the old ideas and Bible teaching was proven to be the best idea in the end. Men akin to God is nothing but a blasphemy, as no man can ever compare himself to God.

By reading the scripture carefully, we'll see how the Earth is mentioned as a face and not a surface. Which means the earth is a flat surface (planar). All other 3D geometric structures, including the sphere, are categorized as surfaces. The face of the earth is mentioned 29 times in the Bible, and not once as the 'surface of the earth'. Therefore, we can safely conclude that the Earth is not a ball and is not moving through space at incredible speeds.

I often wonder how come we did not crash into something else, since we are moving so fast and so randomly. There must be structures out there, like asteroids and clusters of debris standing in our way, and yet we did not run into any of them. Strange, isn't it? As if they get a call right before we pass by and they move out of our way, so we can pass safely.

Copernicus' heliocentric theory suggests that we move around the sun at constant speeds, along with the other planets of the solar system, while the sun is travelling too through the Galaxy at even greater speeds. Plus, the Earth is spinning around its axis, at thousands of miles per hour. Gather the following speeds and see what you get: 1000 miles per hour around its axis, then 67,000 miles per hour around the sun, plus the speed of the sun at 450,000 miles per hour around the center of the galaxy.

These speeds make me dizzy already, and yet, I cannot feel a thing. Every time I go outside, everything looks still to me and I don't feel any dizziness. Mark my words when I tell you that, with such speeds, we would be thrown out of this plane before we could even notice it.

Interesting facts that support the flat earth theory

"Fear before him, all the earth: the world also shall be stable, that it be not moved.: I Chronicles 16:30

"...the world also is stablished, that it cannot be moved." Psalm 93:1

"Who laid the foundations of the earth, that it should not be removed for ever." Psalm 104:5

I would say the Word of God should be enough, when it says, in the Bible, that the earth is still and acts as a footstool for the Almighty. Can you image your footstool flying around your living room? That would not be a very relaxing evening to say the least.

The Earth is still and the 240+ verses, starting with Genesis, are a testimony to this reality that there isn't one verse to support movement of any kind. Yet there are people who choose to doubt the teachings of the Bible. They are not fully convinced by either geocentric or heliocentric paradigms, therefore we are here to clarify some issues and prove the earth is not a globe, but rather a flat surface and we're going to use the 'laws' of physics to disprove the Copernican theory. Yes, the same laws of physics supposed to dethrone the Bible in favor of Scientism (the much-desired new world religion).

Now, you should read the next few paragraphs carefully, and you will understand that I am right about it, and there are literally dozens, if not hundreds, of scientific proofs disproving the spinning ball theory, and yet our textbooks keep presenting the same spinning theory to our children, as if it were an undisputable truth.

The water is our greater ally in this battle, because water will always seek level, a place to rest. Just try to apply water to a round object and see if there is any way that you can make it stick to that surface (unless you mixed it with glue or something). Water will never rest on a ball, regardless of its size, let alone a spinning one that rotates around its axis at incredible speeds (mentioned already, 1000 miles per hour around the equator).

Scientism keeps pushing this idea under our noses, that, since the earth is 25,000 miles in circumference, the water can stay in its place without any issues. Really? So much water being held in place at terrible speeds just like that? In this situation, even Newton's gravitational theory does not work anymore. It is impossible to hold so much water on a spherical object, since water will try to reach the lowest places, so the curvature theory just does not work.

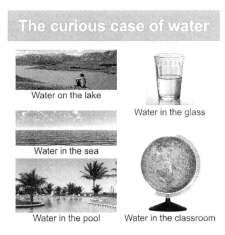

Imagine the oceans of the world splashing apart, just like Moses did with the Red Sea, with water flowing separately on both sides of the highest point of the curvature. Cool picture, isn't it? Well, it would be, but with a round earth, the peak of the curvature is everywhere, depending on where you stand... So, we have a little bit of a problem here, as you can see.

The next argument we are going to take here is related to the previous one, as it regards the oceans and seas of the world and how we can always observe a level horizon. If you have the possibility, just go to the beach one day and look towards the horizon. Regardless of how wide your view is and how far into the distance you can see, you will not observe any curvature. People have also tried doing the same thing from a great altitude by using helium balloons and professional cameras, and they still could not see any curvature. The horizon always stays flat, even when filmed from a 20 mile altitude (like three times the altitude that commercial planes fly at nowadays).

The reality we can see with our own eyes is obvious and is just one, and yet, Scientism is trying to convince us that we are living on a relatively round planet that's spinning through space. Now, I wonder how successful they are, because we can see in society a trend, where we choose to believe an 'established' truth, instead of trusting our own senses.

I often heard discussions about the satellite antennas, and how they work by picking up the TV signal coming from satellites that revolved around the earth, on and on. Well, if they were picking up their signal from moving satellites, then why isn't your antenna moving with the satellite (if it could ever do such a thing)? How does it pick up the signal, when the satellite is on the other side of the earth, then?

You see, things don't work like that, and you're getting your signal from tall ground antennas. Just think of how many radio towers we have. The principle is the same. You don't need a satellite to send wireless signals, just a bunch of ground antennas placed at strategic points along the route and you can do the trick simply.

We often think we know how things work, but we believe the complicated version we are being shown, when in fact, the reality is much simpler... Too simple to be believed sometimes, don't you think? Yes, we have been led to believe that the truth is always complicated, when in fact, the path to the truth is always the shortest of them all.

Scientism managed to fool us into believing our own capacity of observation can be relative and subjective, thus, no matter what we see and feel, it can't be right if it does not align with their theories. Are we such fools? I find it hard to believe that we can't see the truth that's standing right in front of our eyes. But, then again, I go back to the same feeling of belonging and acceptance.

If a sufficient number of people have been convinced that the earth is not flat, and a majority agreeing with the round paradigm has been established, the rest of their mission is nothing but a piece of cake. We're inherently afraid of being rejected, therefore, we'll keep our mouths shut in front of the charade. People might not choose sides but choosing to stay neutral in this matter is harming to the truth, because the number of those brave enough to expose the lie is limited, therefore, their impact is also limited.

Now, let's talk a bit about how submarines, planes and other types of aircraft don't need to adjust their trajectory for each square mile (the well-known 8 inches per mile squared). Also, while flying or going under water, the pilots of both planes and submarines don't have to adjust for the 'supposed' curvature or movement of the earth.

These pure facts are the ultimate proof that our world, the earth, is fixed, stationary, and does not move at hundreds and thousands of miles an hour. Why are these aspects discarded when a debate over the shape and motion of the earth is started? Why are all of these people choosing to close their eyes to the truth? I guess we heard so many times how the earth is round that we find it hard to believe otherwise.

Sometimes, dismantling a lie can be harder than initially building it, and that's because these lies have the tendency to creep under people's skin. With time, the lie becomes a part of the human culture, until you cannot distinguish between the truth and the lie anymore. Today, it's even easier to accomplish the goal of fooling people. Our eyes are the mirrors to our souls and they help us navigate through the world. More than 80% of the information about our environment and life is gathered with the help of our eyes.

By assaulting our senses with countless images of the round earth throughout the media, Scientism managed to paralyze our capacity to analyze and disseminate. It's clear to me now that they have understood how pushing our senses to the limit will only work in their favor. I know for a fact that we are not at the end of the game, by far, we still have our chance to break out of this slumber.

Try doing an experiment where you exclude all media influence from your life. Cut out social media or whatever else that's keeping you busy and focus on living your life. Use your eyes and judge things without thinking of what others might say or think. Trust me when I tell you that you have no idea how much we are censoring ourselves these days. You might feel the earth is flat, because that's what you're seeing and that's how you experience life, on a flat level, but where's the courage to admit it in front of everyone else?

It becomes easier when you stop thinking of what other people are thinking. Just look at the facts, analyze the data and the world, and draw a conclusion for yourself. It really does not matter what other people say if you know the truth. Your life will not be influenced in any way if people do not agree with your view. All that matters is what you think and at the end of the day, the truth. And the funny thing is that the truth is never complicated, and you can just observe it with your own eyes.

Now, let's look at some of the greatest infrastructural works, such as bridges and railroads. They range from miles, to hundreds of miles, and even thousands of miles in length and not once did the blueprints of those projects consider the curvature of the earth, not even when built over the water. Engineers and architects always designed and built their constructions following a flat model of the earth, where they did not have to compensate for those 8 inches (for each square mile).

It's funny how the people who are actually doing the work and would have to deal with the motion of the earth and the round ball model never mention the fact that they have to make adjustments. Scientism, on the other hand, full of theorists and not a single practical professional, keeps making claims it has never proved in its life. From Copernicus to Newton to Einstein, all of these great scientists kept making claims about the world and the universe, but they never saw any of it.

To me, this is a paradox, filled with ignorance. You can't just dream about something during the night and then come out to the light of the day and pretend you have invented/discovered a new physical law or God knows what. We are not talking about literature here! If members of scientism come up with all sorts of untested and unproven ideas and claim them to be universal truths, then there's something wrong with us, if we accept them without a shred of doubt.

Theories like Einstein's relativity and Newton's theory of gravity are nothing but theories that prove nothing. There is no way of testing these ideas, because we do not have the devices to do so and we don't even possess all the data or facts. Recently, it was discovered that light can be bent and there are certainly other forces in the universe faster than light. So, what should we believe now? Who's right and who's wrong in this race for the truth?

Just imagine how it must have been hundreds of years back, when Newton came up with the idea of gravity. We could barely look at the sky with some rudimentary telescopes, let alone test anything, and yet, it was accepted.

While studying history and Scientism's relation with it, I realized how the people who came up with an idea first were considered right. It did not matter how outlandish and impossible to prove that idea was, it was still largely accepted, if there were not 'competitors' for the throne. Just like that, gravity was accepted, because no one else shouted loud enough to contest Newton's idea.

It did not matter that Newton proposed a hoax to the world. It 'sounded' scientific, thus, why not accept it? There was no better offer on the table at that time. Over the years, people started doubting gravity and how it affects us and the world, and tried to prove how other principles, such as density and buoyancy, are responsible for the governance of things. These two principles, easily provable, are, in fact, the natural regulars that God created to determine what rises and what falls, depending on the density of the medium.

You can do this experiment at home. It's easy to prove how different things float in different environments, depending on their density. All you need is a transparent jar and some liquids, such as water, oil, honey, milk, and so on, and then, you can place objects made up of different materials (relative weights) and you can observe how each of them floats in the environment that suits it best.

There is no need for gravity here, because there is no gravity that pulls people and things down to the earth. We keep seeing, in documentaries and TV shows, how much thrust a rocket needs to 'defeat' earth's gravity and how costly each flight is, but then I ask myself, why are they pushing this lie still, when there is nowhere else to go? Our world is this one, in front of our eyes, and there is no 'other place', no matter how much billionaire philanthropists and scientists insist we need to grab our stuff and move out.

"He unleashes his lightning beneath the whole heaven and sends it to the ends of the earth." Job 37:3

With a round model, the world would have no end, and we'd be spinning round and round in our attempts to find that end. Yet, the Bible clearly tells us that God created Earth as a finite surface, with palpable ends. This situation would only be possible if the Earth is flat.

The Bible is full of references to the flat model, and we can see it from Genesis chapter one (when God speaks about the face of the earth and how he moved over the face of the waters/ face means flat, leveled) to Revelation.

"... I saw the four angels standing on the four corners of the earth, holding the four winds of the earth..." Revelation 7:1

Square and Stationary Earth by Orlando Ferguson 1893

This clear depiction of the world, compared with a regular four walled room, shows us how the earth is structured. With the angels standing on the four corners of the world, meaning that we have four distinct quarters composing the earth as a whole.

Therefore, we have Antarctica, which is depicted as a separate continent at the base of the planetary model, that stands as the barrier at the edge of the world. You probably did not think of Antarctica as a wall, or anything similar, but it acts as a protective boundary. For that reason, the environment has been so hostile there and the temperatures so unforgiving, to keep away the danger. Since life was basically almost impossible for humans and their livestock there, we would not venture so far, because it would endanger our own survival.

Right now, if you paid attention to the media and Hollywood, there are instances in movies and shows where they are throwing us hints about this aspect. We have no idea what lies beyond that barrier, but it's okay, people are not picking up on the hints we are being given at all, so I guess we should not worry about it too much. What we don't know can't hurt us, right? Well, I don't know... I always thought I should know the truth regardless how nasty it was, because knowing gave this peace of mind that nothing else could give me.

The Earth, The Sun & The Moon

We should focus a little bit on the relation between the Earth, the Sun, and the Moon, our light and life givers that are supposed to be hundreds of thousands and millions of miles away. Those millions and billions do not impress me at all, and that's because I know the truth.

The Big Bang cosmology insists in telling us that the earth revolves around the sun, with a small tilt of 23,5 degrees, compared to the orbital axis. For that reason, we are made to believe that we have the seasons as a result, but their explanations end there. Well, I say you should know a few interesting facts about the tilted model and what would happen along the seasons if we were actually spinning around the sun.

With every winter and summer, the ice caps would change their place on the planet, but we don't really see that happening too often, do we? The movement of the ice caps every year would cause a disastrous wobble in Earth's rotation, due to the shifting of weight back and forth, and the axis would constantly change.

I believe that none of us feels this wobble and we are definitely not seeing any ice movement around the globe. That happens because the Sun is the one moving on a pre-established path, as it is placed inside the firmament of the earth, a lot closer than Scientism proclaims.

"...the sun, which is a bridegroom coming out of its chamber, and rejoiceth as a strong man to run a race. His going forth is from the end of the heaven, and his circuit unto the ends of it: and there is nothing hid from the heat thereof." Psalm 19: 4-6

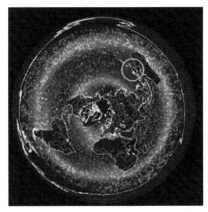

Azimuthal equidistant map water currents projection

Furthermore, to convince yourself, you just need to check the temperature of the oceans of the world and compare it to an azimuthal equidistant map of the world. These types of projections show you exactly how the warmest waters follow the line of the equator (between the tropics), the exact path of the sun. Should this be a coincidence? I don't think so! Nothing in this world happens by coincidence, the way Scientism tries to portray things (with their evolution theories and the laws that supposedly govern this world).

Another interesting aspect that leads us to the conclusion that the earth is flat and the sun is inside the firmament, is the sunsets and the long reflection of the sun's beams. If the earth was indeed spherical and the sun was truly 93 million miles away, you would not see any reflection in the ocean water at sunset, and that's because the rate of drop off would not provide enough surface area and it would angle the sun light away from your eyes. Only on a flat surface can you get such an effect, and we are seeing it every time we look at the ocean, in the evening, on a clear sky.

We've gathered quite a lot of evidence already, and yet, to Scientism, nothing seems to be enough, thus we are not going to stop here, because we have a lot more to cover.

Now, let's look at the Bible and see what the Holy Word of God has to say about this celestial body, which Scientism claims is situated hundreds of thousands of miles away from Earth.

Throughout ancient times, the moon and the sun were regarded as distinct entities in terms of gender. The Sun (Sol) is referred to in the masculine and the moon (luna) is referred to in the feminine. They are not the same. She does not show his light.

"For the stars of heaven and the constellations thereof shall not give their light: the sun shall be darkened in his going forth, and the moon shall not cause her light to shine." Isaiah 13:10

The moon was created by God, as He realized that the night was too dark for man to wander the earth. The moon lights up on its own, despite what Scientism or other 'qualified' people claim, that it's just a reflection of the sun's rays. The moon as an entity is independent and there are numerous verses in the Bible that prove the moon has its own independent source of light.

"Thus saith the LORD, which giveth the sun for a light by day, and the ordinances of the moon and of the stars for a light by night, which divideth the sea when the waves thereof roar; The LORD of hosts is his name." Jeremiah 31:35

When analyzing the spectrum of both lights (sun and moon), we can see how the sun emits a stronger light (you can't look at it without a pair of sun glasses). The sun has a color temperature of 5,800K, visually warm, ranging from warm white to yellow and is physically warm. The moon, on the other hand, has a color temperature of 4,000K, is visually cold, ranges from silver pale to white and is physically cold.

Again, the atmosphere reason as to why the blue spectrum of the sun's light does not really stand tall. Scientists claim the blue spectrum is dispersed high up in the atmosphere, but it only happens in the case of the sun, while the moon looks like it comes from a different world.

The truth is simple! The Bible underlines the purpose of both heavenly bodies and you don't have to look anywhere else for any explanation.

"Thus saith the LORD, which giveth the sun for a light by day, and the ordinances of the moon and of the stars for a light by night." Jeremiah 31:35

When God created the Sun, he saw its usefulness during the day, but man, beast, and every plant needed the night to rest and prepare for the next day. The moon was created to fill that dark void, but it could not be the same as the sun, since we would not have had night, in that case. Each heavenly body (Sun and Moon) is special and has its own purpose, but at the same time, they have something in common: both the moon and the sun are situated inside the firmament!

"And God made two great lights; the greater light to rule the day, and the lesser light to rule the night: he made the stars also. And God set them in the firmament of the heaven to give light upon the earth, And to rule over the day and over the night, and to divide the light from the darkness: and God saw that it was good. And the evening and the morning were the fourth day." Genesis 1: 16-19

A step back into history~ the origins of the round earth ideology.

Around two millennia ago, a man called Eratosthenes, decided to do an experiment, where he measured the angles of the shadows of two obelisks in two different cities. It happened on the summer solstice and judging by the difference between the angles of the shadows (7.2 degrees) and the position/ distance between the two cities, he concluded that this must be the effect of earth's curvature. Thinking the sun rays must be vertical, which is not actually true, and the fact that the sun must be millions of miles away, he used the process of triangulation and determined the earth's circumference at 24,662 miles, a value that is close to the modern measurements of 24,900 miles.

Eratosthenes experiment

Now, let's turn our heads in the flat earth direction and observe how the same triangulation works perfectly well, but, in this case, we cut the million miles from the distance between the sun and the earth and place the sun closer to us. By analyzing the flat model, where the sun follows a path with limited latitude variation, the results we get are rather encouraging, and by using the same shadow variations and the triangulation method, we get that the Sun is only 3000 miles above our heads with a circumference of only 32 miles.

By using a sextant, you will reach the same conclusions, that testify for the flat earth model. 38 miles for the sun's diameter and 3,100 miles for the distance between the sun and Earth. The sextant isn't a very complicated tool, and anyone could learn to use it, thus you could do this experiment on your own.

Some interesting facts:

All the elite world leaders know the truth about the fact that the earth is flat, and yet, for some reason, they decided to keep the rest of us in the dark. Probably, some of them have seen things the rest of the world has no idea exist in the first place, and that's why they feel privileged. They feel like they are above everyone else.

Inside this lie, there are little glimpses of truth, sometimes hidden in an occult aura, and sometimes thrown at us in plain sight, as if they are trying to laugh at us. Maybe they are trying to test us to see if we have any reaction at all. We shall have one, one day, I am certain of it, and I would kill to be there and to see their faces when they realize that people have finally woken up.

After World War II ended, a few agencies were created to maintain world peace and followed the development of the world, following the greatest conflagration of all times. One of these institutions, designed to have a key role, was the United Nations (UN). To me, this is the precursor of world government and was created exactly for this purpose and this purpose alone. They did not show off from the beginning, because they did not know what people's reaction would be, but, little by little, they started showing their teeth.

Their intent is clear, but now let's focus a little bit on their flag and how it depicts the flat earth model. The design of the flag is copied 100%, except for Antarctica, which has been replaced by two olive branches (supposed to represent peace). I don't know what you see, but, to me, this is the perfect representation of the world, exactly the way each map should look like, and they put that map on the flag of the future 'world government'.

If you're thinking this must be some sort of coincidence, that these people chose the flag randomly, I am telling you it's not! Scientism does not leave anything to chance. These folks don't play with Goddess Fortuna, and always plan every single move very carefully. If you think they have made a mistake, it's nothing but calculated bait they are throwing at us. The UN flag falls in the same category, as they put the flat earth map on it intentionally.

It's like they are trying to associate the flag with the UN and nothing else, and it looks like they have succeeded to some extent, because if you show ten people the map and ask them what it is, more than half will tell you 'the UN flag' almost instantly. It's painful to see how some people have lost connection with the origin of things, but I don't blame them in any way. We were all born and raised in this toxic environment and it is our duty, those of us who have opened our eyes already, to help and direct the 'lost sheep' in the right direction. I know the process will be long and painful, but I am willing to invest every drop of sweat and energy into this endeavor.

Enoch and his accounts of heaven and earth

The book of Enoch is not part of the canonical Bible, but it is considered a credible source, since Jesus himself mentions it when he talked to Sadducees, thus confirming the validity of Enoch's writings. In case you want to study the Book of Enoch yourself, you should keep in mind that only the book under the name 1 Enoch or the Ethiopian book of Enoch is the real one. The rest are only approximate renderings and are subject to interpretation.

So, now that we managed to clear that up, we should delve more into detail, since the book of Enoch is an incredible source of truth, filled with exact details and facts that would baffle anyone. The style in which the book is written is rough and direct and tells things exactly for what they are. No interpretation or metaphor. This was probably one of the reasons why it was not included in the canon, since it stirred emotions of great intensity that would probably scare people. Enoch was the 7[th man] after Adam, living in a time, when was still wandering on the face of the earth, and people's connections with God were stronger than they are now. His accounts depict the earth, the sun, the moon, and the stars differently from what we are used to today, and it's important to understand that he is one of those men who have seen things with their own eyes, no theorizing or interpretation.

"...I saw the ends of the earth whereon the heaven rests, and the portals of the heaven open. And I saw how the stars of the heaven come forth, and I counted the portals out of which they proceed, and wrote down all their outlets, of each individual star by itself, accounting to their number and their names, their courses and their position, and their times and their months, as Uriel the holy angel who was with me showed me. He showed all things to me and wrote them down for me: also their names he wrote for me, and their laws and companies." 1 Enoch 33:2-4

We see how Enoch clearly speaks about the end of the earth. In this situation, the round earth model is practically impossible. Enoch goes on with his statements and explains to us what stands beyond the firmament and the sky we can all see. He speaks about a place situated beyond the abyss, where there is no firmament, a horrible place, a waste land.

"And beyond that abyss I saw a place which had no firmament of the heaven above, and no firmly founded earth beneath it: here was no water upon it, and no birds, but it was a waste and horrible place. I saw there seven stars like great burning mountains, and to me, when I inquired regarding them, the angel said: "This place is the end of the heaven and earth: this has become a prison for the stars and the host of heaven. And the stars which roll over the fire are they which have transgressed the commandment of the Lord in the beginning of their rising, because they did not come forth at their appointed times. And He was wroth with them and bound them till the time when their guilt should be consummated (even) for ten thousand years." 1 Enoch 18:12

If we follow this paragraph closely, we can see how Enoch mentions the 'water upon it'. We know from Genesis in the Bible, that God separated the waters from the waters when creating the Earth, and now we have the waters above the firmament and the waters below (as in the oceans and seas of the world).

Enoch's statement strengthens again the claims of the Bible and reinforces the flat model.

Another interesting aspect Enoch mentions is about the 7 disobedient stars, who are punished for not coming forth at their designated time. Right now, we officially have 8 planets in our solar system, and if we exclude earth, we have 7. See the resemblance of the numbers? How could they have known thousands of years ago, when they had no telescopes or other magnifying tools? They could not see the distant planets with a naked eye, and yet, they knew about their existence. Instead of planets, Enoch regards the 'wandering stars' as living entities, associated with angels, entities that could reason and think for themselves, since they were capable of disobeying God's command.

In a way, the wandering stars are similar to Satan (Lucifer, aka the morning star). Fallen angels, who thought they could be greater than god, and for that reason, they were punished and sent to a waste land, beyond heaven and earth. A hell, in simpler terms, where the 7 stars are bound to wander in solitude for thousands of years, until they finally 'served their sentence'.

Blasting the firmament (or trying to, at least)

As soon as World War II ended, and humankind got hold of some powerful nuclear weapons, something interesting started happening. It was clear that, with the development of jet planes, people got the opportunity to fly higher and faster, and thus, they probably started seeing some interesting things. Unfortunately, for the rest of us, with all these military operations being highly classified, we did not get to hear too much about it.

Even today, we don't know anything real about those missions, just the names and the fact that some 'bombs exploded' for no logical reason, apparently. At the end of 1950's and the beginning of the 1960's, after the Antarctic treaty was signed, the United States began blasting the atmosphere with a series of powerful nuclear weapons (The soviets accompanied them, if you had any doubts about it).

Operation Fishbowl preparations on Johnston Island 1962

Operation Fishbowl is probably the most famous of them all. Fishbowl, huh? A quite predestined name, don't you think? It looks to me like these explosions were nothing but the desperate attempt of a fish to break the bowl it was living in. With the flat earth model, the firmament acts like a sealing glass, and it looks like our people tried to break through it and see what's beyond it.

By reading the Bible, we can see mankind dreamed of reaching the heavens before. The proud people of Babylon, seen as one of the greatest nations on earth, decided they had reached the rank of Gods themselves and it was time to meet the creator and see the place where he dwelled. A common language, a common law for the whole known world and all the riches a man could dream of, plus all the decadence and vice that followed.

"Now the whole world had one language and a common speech. As people moved eastward, they found a plain in Shinar and settled there.

They said to each other, "Come, let's make bricks and bake them thoroughly." They used brick instead of stone, and tar for mortar. Then they said, "Come, let us build ourselves a city, with a tower that reaches to the heavens, so that we may make a name for ourselves; otherwise we will be scattered over the face of the whole earth."

But the Lord came down to see the city and the tower the people were building. The Lord said, "If as one people speaking the same language they have begun to do this, then nothing they plan to do will be impossible for them. Come, let us go down and confuse their language so they will not understand each other."

So the Lord scattered them from there over all the earth, and they stopped building the city. That is why it was called Babel— because there the Lord confused the language of the whole world. From there the Lord scattered them over the face of the whole earth." Genesis 11:1-9

Again, we find the reference to the 'face' of the earth, meaning a flat surface, but what I find more intriguing is the fact that we faced the same situation thousands of years ago. It looks like man has always dreamed to reach the heavens before dying a natural death. A global government (an empire having the known world under its control) and a common language, like what English is for us today. I am sure that in 100 years everyone, will be speaking English, while leaving their ancestral languages behind. Kind of the same thing that happened in the Spanish empire in South and Central America.

At that point, we'll be a sort of modern Babylon, sharing the same satanic ideas and principles, and little by little, we can see that some of us have started rebelling against God right now. The worst part is that they're trying to drag us into this unholy battle of theirs too.

I wonder what will happen to us this time, when facing God's wrath. We have conquered the entire face of the earth, and clearly, we have nowhere else to be scattered to. This is just a thought of mine, anyway. If 3,000 years ago, building a brick tower was vicious attempt at reaching the sky, the intention mattered the most, and I am afraid that nowadays, with our technology and advanced gadgets, we can do a lot more. Blasting those nuclear weapons into the firmament, I believe is the modern attempt at reaching the heavens. I don't think, though, that anything made by man will ever be able to destroy something created by God.

If we think we can compare ourselves (with our little bombs) to God, then we are terrible mistaken. I am sure the people in charge of the Fishbowl mission realized the futility of their struggle, and after a couple of failed attempts, they stopped blasting nuclear weapons at all. The only achievement (a negative one, of course) was that those explosions contaminated the atmosphere and the clouds, thus, harmed us in ways we can't imagine.

"For all the nations have drunk of the wine of the passion of her immorality, and the kings of the earth have committed acts of immorality with her, and the merchants of the earth have become rich by the wealth of her sensuality." And he cried out with a mighty voice, saying, "Fallen, fallen is Babylon the great! She has become a dwelling place of demons and a prison of every unclean spirit, and a prison of every unclean and hateful bird. and the light of a lamp will not shine in you any longer; and the voice of the bridegroom and bride will not he heard in you any longer; for your merchants were the great men of the earth, because all the nations were deceived by your sorcery." Revelation 18: 1-4

No wonder the Bible mentions Babylon in Revelation and how the people of the world will eventually fall into the same ancestral sin of vanity. Scientism is nothing but a different face of the same phenomenon, as it teaches us and pushes us, little by little, away from God.

The round earth, the mocking addressed to the Bible, all the blasphemies with the evolution theories and how man evolved from monkeys. What's next? What kind of outlandish idea or theory should we expect next, because I feel like we have seen it all already?

It is quite clear that the Babylonian-style world order is on their menu. Round or flat, they're planning on making it their own, regardless of our presence, thoughts, or preferences. That they are concerned, I'm sure, that they will just say |get out of here or die, if you don't like our rules." And God, where is he in this equation? What place is left for the Almighty, the one who created everything, including us? I see how they see no need for God, or for his miracles, as Scientism is planned to be the next religion for the 3rd millennium.

I could not help noticing Ronald Reagan's words during a press conference, after a meeting he had with Gorbachev. There, he said with a big smile on his face, that he had a revelation, noticing how easily people would unite, when we all face an external threat. All of our differences and grudges, some that lasted for centuries, would disappear in an instant, and we would unite under the same cause... or the same world order.

Men like him, or Bush Sr., are rather scary, because they are not ashamed of their mission and the evil they were perpetrating in the world. They are rather proud of their role and would even want to be applauded for it. I am disgusted by such men, who care nothing for their kin and would not flinch for a split second, even if they knew that millions had died because of them. Men like Reagan are clearly devoid of soul or any trace of humanity.

There is, indeed, an external threat, but I am not talking about aliens or god knows what, coming from light years away. No, I am talking about something much more 'familiar', the embodiment of evil itself. Satan is our greatest threat and it can be considered both external and internal, if you wish, because it works its evilness among people and through people. This is the enemy we should all unite against, but Scientism does not want us to fight the real enemy. They want to chase wild geese, while they keep working on their agenda.

"Keep them divided, and even better, against each other, and you will surely win!" This age-old tactic has worked so well throughout the years. Men against men have used it with success, and now, Satan is using it against us all. I feel both anger and pity for those who think they are working in their own interest, while doing the work of the devil. They are not condemning only their own souls, but through their actions, they are sealing the fates of the rest of us. For that reason, we need to fight back and prove that God is more powerful than Satan, and through Him, we will prevail.

Is the earth actually rotating? Not really!

We mentioned previously how the Bible tells us that the earth is stationary and all the other elements in the sky are moving around us, but I want to make things even clearer and prove to you that the earth is motionless. Yes, there are ways by which we can prove the Earth is not moving at all, but it looks like Scientism decided to as

First of all, I want to talk to you about the Coriolis effect a little bit. The Coriolis force is described by Wikipedia as an inertial force acting on the objects that are in motion, in relation to a certain rotating reference frame. In our case, the frame is the earth. If the frame has a clockwise rotation, the force will act to the left, and if the frame rotates counter-clockwise, then the force will act to the right.

So, let's analyze the Coriolis effect on bullets, if there is any effect at all. If I were to shoot a bullet north or south, following the Coriolis Effect, I should miss the target by a couple of hundred meters. This should be the natural effect on a spinning ball, since the earth is supposed to spin around its axis at a top speed of 1000 miles per hour, but this does not happen at all, regardless of which altitude you shoot that bullet. This is reality and the facts are registered in the Army ballistic tables. It's not something I made up right now, thus, you can check the facts for yourself, if you're curious enough.

And this is just the beginning of our explanation. Now, think of parachutes, planes, skydivers, and other freely moving objects in the sky. Not even once has the movement of the earth been noticed, and that's because it is stationary. Any perceived Coriolis Effect is caused by other factors, such as wind, inertia, or the parachute itself, etc.

I bet you have all seen the moment when a parachute opens. You have seen the motion and how the wind stops the man from falling at a fast speed. And yet, have you ever seen the parachute moving violently right or left, depending on the hemisphere? I have not seen any effect of that sort, and it's weird not to see it, since the earth is spinning at incredible speeds. The effect should be sudden and violent, but all we can see once the parachute opens is a smooth slide, guided by the one who is controlling the flight.

No skydiver takes into consideration the speed of Earth's rotation when trying to hit a target. The only aspects considered are wind speed and altitude. Back in October 2012, Felix Baumgartner, a professional skydiver, jumped from the highest point (39 kilometers), right at the edge of the stratosphere. The whole jump was filmed with a professional camera, and no one could see any movement of the earth. Plus, considering the spinning speed, Felix should have landed, hundreds of kilometers away from his designated target, and yet, managed to land where he proposed with no problems, and without taking into account any rotation of the earth. What does this tell us? That we have been lied to, probably? That even right now, we are living a lie? Most certainly!

Scientism tries to explain the Earth's rotation by telling us how the oceans are bulged around the equator, and how there's more water in those regions, due to the speed of the rotation, but they are not telling us the whole truth. In this scenario they are proposing, the water should have collected around the equator and spun off a long time ago, and yet, we see our oceans filled with millions of cubic tons of water.

What's holding the water on earth then? As mentioned previously, the water will always seek to find its own level and since the earth is a flat surface (with mountains and hills, of course), the water has no problem staying in its place.

In case you are still having doubts about it, just take a wet tennis ball and spin it, and you will see how the water gathers at the 'equator' of the ball, and then is pushed out, due to the spinning motion. In  just a few seconds, the ball will be almost dry, and so should the Earth be, if it were a spinning ball going at incredible speeds through empty space.

Another experiment you could easily try at night involves the stars and a clear sky. If you try taking a picture of the sky, you will see how the stars can be seen clearly, and, with a decent camera, you can take outstanding pictures. How is this possible? If the Earth were to move at 1000 miles per hour, all you should see is a nasty blur, of which you could not discern almost anything. Just think what you would get if you tried to take a picture, while riding in a car, that goes at 150 miles an hour or even 100 miles an hour. Your camera will not be able to picture anything clearly and you'd even have problems focusing on some specific object.

We have all these arguments at hand, yet Scientism still dismisses the possibility that our Earth is a stationary body, while the rest of the celestial figures are moving around. Why can't they simply accept the facts, the reality that is so much closer to us than all their theories and equations?

You might be surprised, but I am not the only one, or the first one, who embarks on such an endeavor. In the last century, countless people have fought the Scientism chimera, but they were defeated or condemned to oblivion, regardless of how famous or intelligent they were. It does not mean we should give up. On the contrary, we should keep on fighting, because we have the Lord on our side and we'll be victorious in the end.

Nikola Tesla was one of those men who saw the error of science and the path that the people involved in Scientism were walking down. Tesla is probably the greatest scientist (true scientist) and inventor the world has ever seen! Einstein or Edison pale in comparison to Tesla, who was simply the master of electricity and understood the importance of the electric current and force fields in relation to Earth's existence, as well as the natural phenomena we see all around us.

This man was so ahead of his time and so focused on the true nature of science, that Scientism pushed him out of the way, little by little, until he was almost forgotten. Textbooks barely talk about him and his amazing achievements (I wonder why) and they glorify individuals, who had nothing to do with true science. I guess Napoleon was right when he said that history is nothing, but a fable written by the winners. If you lose the battle, you lose your voice, and I am not referring to actual war now, because there is a war going on in Science now, one directed against us.

Tesla Quote:

"Today's scientists have substituted mathematics for experiments, and they wander off through equation after equation, and eventually build a structure, which has no relation to reality."

Tesla died on January 7th, 1943, thus, almost 80 years ago, and even then, he saw the workings of Scientism and how these people were trying to distort reality by lying to our faces. A highly intelligent man, involved with science, he quickly discovered the errors of their judgment (intentional, most likely) and tried to uncover their lies, but he was alone, against a machinery that included vast financial resources and a majority willing to compromise anything in order to keep their lie alive.

Tesla Quote:

"Only the existence of a field of force can account for the motions of the bodies as observed, and its assumption dispenses with space curvature. All literature on this subject is futile and destined to oblivion. So are all attempts to explain the workings of the universe without recognizing the existence of the ether and the indispensable function it plays in the phenomena."

Again, Tesla sees how Scientism tries to explain things the wrong way and convince the rest of us, at the same time, that they are right. The Ether, Tesla speaks about is nothing but the divine energy created by God, that simply animates the world. Everything would be dead, including us, if it were not for the breath of God that turned clay into living flesh.

The earth itself is alive, even if Scientism is trying to depict it as a random stone, flying through space, ready to be exploited and poisoned at our will. Every living creature and plant in this world was created along with the earth. We might not realize it yet, but we are hurting the Earth in ways we can't understand. Our lack of understanding comes from the philosophy that Scientism has preached over the last few centuries.

We were fooled to believe, at a social level, to regard ourselves as separate from the rest of the world, as if we were against the world, but it's not actually like that. It is us with the world, in symbiosis, and we should guard and protect it, instead of trashing it. There is no other earth, regardless of how much Scientism tries to convince us that we have thousands of 'super earths' at our disposal, only in our galaxy and other billions of them around the universe.

God created us to rule over the earth, but rule, in this case, means responsibility not recklessness.

Then God said, "Let Us make man in Our image, according to Our likeness; and let them rule over the fish of the sea and over the birds of the sky and over the cattle and over all the earth, and over every creeping thing that creeps on the earth." Genesis 1:26

Why is Antarctica so special?

If we look on the map, we can see that Antarctica is portrayed as the southernmost continent in the world. With a supposed surface of 14,000,000 square kilometers, it is the fifth largest continent in the world. Being covered by snow and ice 12 months a year, Antarctica is one of the driest and most hostile environments on Earth, for that reason, it was only discovered in the 19th century.

Life for human beings was practically impossible here, due to the low temperatures and scarce wildlife (only penguins and seals). Therefore, Antarctica remained relatively unexplored for the next hundred years. People did not have the technology and ships to perform safe expeditions, as a result, the interest in this new continent was rather low.

All that lack of interest towards Antarctica vanished at the beginning of the 20th century, when the English Government, through Ernest Shackleton, started their first Antarctic mission in 1907, which lasted until 1909. Shackleton and his crew managed to get to 112 miles from the South Pole.

The most interesting aspect about this mission was the name they chose for their ship: Nimrod. This was the man under whose rule the construction of the tower of Babel was attempted. Does this ring a bell to you already? I bet it does! We all know the purpose of the tower of Babel was to take man to the heavens, but their attempt ended in failure and they were scattered upon the face of the earth, never speaking the same language again.

"And they said, Go to, let us build us a city a tower, whose top may reach unto heaven; and let us make us a name, lest we be scattered abroad upon the fact of the whole earth.... Therefore is the name of it called Babel; because the Lord did there confound the language of all the earth: and from thence did the Lord scatter them abroad upon the face of all the earth." Genesis 11:4-9

Was the name of the ship chosen randomly? I don't think so, as the bloodlines of western Europe are strongly connected to those of the ancient empires. They knew the meaning of the name and probably thought to bring a tribute to their ancestor, as they were finally about to reach out unto the heavens.

We never seem to learn our lesson, and after we get punished for our disobedience, we keep our heads down for a while, only to try and raise them higher later. We did not obey God in the garden of Eden, when Eve corrupted Adam to eat from the forbidden tree.

"Now the serpent was more crafty than any other beast of the field that the Lord God had made. He said to the woman, "Did God actually say, 'You shall not eat of any tree in the garden'?" And the woman said to the serpent, "We may eat of the fruit of the trees in the garden, but God said, 'You shall not eat of the fruit of the tree that is in the midst of the garden, neither shall you touch it, lest you die.'" But the serpent said to the woman, "You will not surely die. For God knows that when you eat of it your eyes will be opened, and you will be like God, knowing good and evil." Genesis 3: 1-24

We died, indeed, after Eve took the first bite from the forbidden fruit, as we lost eternity. We did not gain anything, except for pain and suffering. Evilness started creeping under our skin, right after we were banished from the garden of Eden, and we can see how much we hate each other (pushed from behind by Satan, who rejoices in his achievement).

"Cain spoke to Abel his brother. And when they were in the field, Cain rose up against his brother Abel and killed him." Genesis 4: 8

This is the perfect example of how jealousy and envy have affected our existence, right from the beginning.

Satan never ceased in his attempts at corrupting us, at making us disobedient towards God, and the garden episode was only the beginning. The tower of Babel was yet another instance, where humans were convinced they could reach the level of God, even though we are mere mortals. With the Antarctic expedition, the process had started again, as we started thinking that, with our science, we can achieve anything, even break into the kingdom of God.

Our tools and weapons are useless in front of God, and yet, we seem to never learn our place. The earth is our home and yet we keep wanting to break out and look for other worlds. Our age-old dream has always been to reach the heavens, but are we worthy? Are we virtuous enough for such a privilege? I think we should look at ourselves first and try to please God more, before we break in through the back door like burglars.

The United States of America decided to mount a series of Antarctic expeditions, all led by admiral Richard E. Byrd. The missions themselves were shrouded in mystery and the large public did not find out too much about what Byrd discovered on the frozen 'continent'. All three missions took place between the two world wars, the first one in 1924, the second one in 1928 and the third one in 1938, right before World War II broke out.

The official claim about Byrd's missions was that he and his crew were sent on an exploration mission, as Antarctica was highly unknown to humanity. Previously, people had barely scratched the surface, and the few times that they had actually reached Antarctica, they only set foot on the beaches and the areas around them, since going inland was considered too dangerous, deadly, actually.

Towards the end of the war, the Nazis embarked on complex expeditions to Antarctica. as they were developing their first flying saucers (Rundflugzeug, Feurerball, Diskus, Haunebu, V7). It's highly known that the Nazis were involved with occult knowledge, as they had sent their officers around the world to gather this sort of ancient knowledge, even before the war broke out. The flag of the Nazis is the ultimate proof of their occult agenda, as it comes from the Indian mythology (slightly modified, of course), as the symbol of eternity.

For some reason, all countries that dreamt of world domination came to Antarctica (Americans, Russians, Germans). It looks like there is something there that we know nothing of, but that draws people like a magnet. At first glance, a frozen continent with barely any resources and the worst living conditions would be the last choice for anyone, and yet, people deeply rooted in the occult were determined to get to the 'bottom' of things, against all odds.

It is unclear what the Nazis accomplished, while they stayed in Antarctica, but right after the war ended, and the peace treaties were in place, the United States of America mounted the most complex and impressive Antarctic mission of all time. In 1946, the same Admiral Richard E. Byrd began a campaign that looked more like a war declaration than an exploration mission. During operation High Jump, Admiral Byrd had USS Mount Olympus under his command, along with the aircraft carrier, USS Philippine Sea, plus 13 US Navy support ships, six helicopters, six flying boats, two seaplane tenders, and fifteen other aircraft. The number of personnel reached 4000.

Doesn't this look to you like it's too much gear and people for an exploration mission? Especially when we are talking about an uninhabited continent? To me, it looks like they were preparing to face something, fight someone, because otherwise, you would not take so much military equipment with you. Again, the results of this mission are shrouded in mystery, but later, rumors popped up, where Admiral Byrd claimed that he had found the entrance to a hollow earth.

The man clearly saw something, but I am sure he did not know exactly what he saw, especially when he claimed that giants were living in those places, creatures that lived for hundreds of years and even more.

I strongly believe that the US government had its hints, when preparing this mission, and the extent of their weaponry leads me to believe that they did not know exactly what they were going to meet once they advanced inland. With all the lies and smokescreens, members of Scientism and government know exactly what the truth is, but they are trying to keep it all to themselves, probably thinking that their power and stature will crumble, if everyone else found out what lied beyond the icy walls of Antarctica.

The ice is clearly placed there in such great amounts to scare us and push us away (there is nothing stronger than our survival instinct), but now, with our technology, we can defeat those wretched conditions and see what's beyond the first ice wall.

Should we all see what's out there? I believe we should, if you ask me, because we would finally have a well-deserved rest as a society and humanity. Once we witnessed the might of God's creation, all religious conflicts would disappear and all the disputes and scheming that go on around the world daily would also disappear.

"He hath compassed the waters with bounds, until the day and night come to an end." Job 26: 10

Isn't this clear enough? The world does not have an edge, but it does have a boundary, that's meant to keep us in (probably protected from any external influences, the way Reagan wanted, of course). Antarctica is not actually a continent, but rather a ring of ice that surrounds the Earth, just like a fence.

Through the word 'compassed', we understand a circle drawn with the compass, which is a flat surface. You cannot draw a sphere with a compass. The purpose of these 'bounds' is to keep the above waters from entering our realm, and probably to keep us from going out, which seems like something we desperately wanted to do, at least some people in our government.

The thirst for power becomes unstoppable, after a certain threshold is conquered, and people want more and more for themselves. It looks like our endeavor did not end as expected, and as soon as Admiral Byrd came back from his expeditions, the general trend regarding Antarctica shifted. From exploring, we jumped to preserving, meaning that no one could set foot on the continent without an authorization. People can visit the beaches of Antarctica even today, but they cannot go any further. Such actions are strictly forbidden, for unknown real reasons, of course (at least officially).

There is something going on around Antarctica, otherwise, we could not explain the rush with which, in 1959, 12 of most powerful countries in the world, signed the Antarctic Treaty, declaring the continent as politically neutral. Countries that were enemies to the death, such as the US and the Soviet Union, fell to terms quite quickly and without too much debate. Other countries were part of the agreement, such as the UK, Australia, and others that were closer to Antarctic region (Argentina, Chile).

With a Cold War at full swing and no notion of environmental issues in mind, people were suddenly hit by a feeling of conservation. I mean, we were burning fossil fuels and coal like madmen, but, at the same time, we were concerned with Antarctica's preservation, for future generations, I guess.

In my opinion, Admiral Byrd and the folks who accompanied him received a warning, when they tried to cross the boundary set by God. They probably thought they could go beyond the firmament through one of the entrances, but as soon as they crossed the limit established for humanity, they were met by God's angels (therefore, Byrd is mentioning the giants). Angels are known to be far larger and greater than any regular men.

Byrd did not see a hollow earth, because the earth is not a sphere. He most likely stepped or tried to get into the next realm. He probably caught glimpses that dazzled his eyes and confused him to some extent, and that's why he thought he was seeing another world.

It was, in fact, the same world, but a different dimension of it, one strictly accessible to God and His angels.

God has sent man to earth in order to grow and to prosper here. We are not meant to leave our garden, while we are still breathing, because we are forbidden, if we have not learned our lessons. The boundaries were set in place, thousands of years ago, and we will never be able to break through, regardless of how much we struggle. I believe we should not even try, since our place is here.

You might be wondering right now, as you are reading these lines, if admitting the flat earth model would have any implications on our lives. After all, we would still have to go to work to earn a living, the mortgage for the house or car still needs to be paid each month, or the gas and electric bills, otherwise, we would have our lights cut off. Life would still be hard for most of us, regardless of whether the earth was round of flat, so why so much hassle to keep us with our heads in the sand?

These would be a few pertinent questions, no doubt, and I have quite the right answer for them. Right now, we live through deceptive times, and throughout history, man fought against deception, but now, with the current technology, the means of the 'con artist' are various and incredible. It all started with the Copernican revolution, 500 years ago, as I told you already, and they perfected their means with every passing moment.

They have built the lie and the so-called science to back up their claims and they are aware that, once they admit the flat earth model is the right model, their paradigm will go down in crumbles. It will happen, because everything they came up with over the years was strongly connected to the previous lie.

First, the flat model will fit the numerous descriptive, special, and directional references in the Bible and this is only the beginning. If the round model is pushed aside, the same will happen with all the theories that followed. Goodbye evolution, Big Bang, or atheism for that matter, and people will understand that there is, in fact, a creator.

Once the people understand that we are living on a flat earth and all we see in the sky are mere projections inside the firmament, the alien propaganda will vanish, as if it never existed in the first place. Without infinite galaxies, stars, and habitable planets, it will be obvious that we will not have any external visits anytime soon.

THE GLOBE

THE FOUNDATION FOR EVOLUTION, THE BIG BANG, ATHESIM, ALIEN SEEDING, PAGANISM, AND THE OCCULT, THE NEW WORLD ORDER, AND SATANIC WORLD CONTROL

THE FLAT EARTH

DESCRIBED IN THE BIBLE, VALIDATES THE BIBLE, SCIENTIFICALLY PROVEN, POINTS TO GOD ALONE AS CREATOR, BLOWS SATAN'S DECEPTIONS WIDE OPEN

NOW DO YOU SEE WHY THEY ARE LYING?

Suddenly, the book of revelation will make much more sense to people, and we will all get a hold of the importance of the Word of God and what is expecting us if we keep living our lives as if there is no judgment day. Once people understand that there will be a judgment day, the morals of the masses will change, because they will certainly know they will be held accountable for their deeds.

The final days will come onto humanity, a moment where every single individual will answer for what they did, while walking on the face of the earth. Most people laugh when hearing such words, because they have been brainwashed by Scientism to think that the Holy Bible is nothing but a collection of fables with no real meaning, but they are wrong. That is exactly what Satan wants from us, to turn our faces away from God and to scoff every time we hear his Holy Word.

"Fear none of those things which thou shalt suffer: behold, the devil shall cast some of you into prison, that ye may be tried; and ye shall have tribulation ten days: be thou faithful unto death, and I will give thee a crown of life." Revelation 2:10

The flat earth is simply the cure to all our struggles and doubts. As soon as people understand and accept the fact that we don't live on a spinning ball, the reality of our stewardship will become more prominent in our minds, and our sense of accountability will take on a different meaning in relation to us and the surrounding environment. The moment people realize that there is no other 'super earth' to go to, once we have trashed this one, our behavior will change, and we'll become more aware of the limited space and time we have.

Now, don't get me wrong. It does not mean that we'll have to live our lives in fear or anything like that, because God created us out of love and not terror. The main point here is that we (the world population) will have to change our ways and adapt to the new reality. The result is obvious, don't you think?

The second this paradigm falls, this false reality will break into pieces and the pedestal on which the ruling class stands right now will shatter right in front of their eyes. The reasons that back their power now will become obsolete, and they will start fading away, in poverty, most likely, and that scares them to death.

They have nothing besides their material possessions that they pride so much. Their gold bars, expensive cars, and paper money will lose their value and they will lose everything in the process. With no god, they are afraid of death too, because they don't have the lord to support and guide them. Just like Judah, these people have traded their souls and their eternity for a bag of gold, and in their selfishness, they want to drag us into their misery too.

The end game for this coming world government is to hand the power over to the antichrist, exactly the way the Bible warns us. The enemy of man knows it is impossible to convince all the leaders of the world to hand him the power, therefore he needs the right conditions for taking over the earth. Evil men will do his bidding, first creating the premise for his domination, but only if we let them achieve that.

We are an integrated part of this world and we play our own role in this game. As soon as more of us become conscious of the reality, the real one, and not the one staged in the studios of Hollywood, then we will start to turn things in our favor. The balance is feeble, and Scientism knows it. For that reason, people involved with it, the so-called scientists and others, are struggling to keep our minds busy and our souls in shackles. Remember, it's all about perception and belief.

"But we are bound to give thanks always to God for you, brethren beloved of the Lord, because God hath from the beginning chosen you to salvation through sanctification of the Spirit and belief of the truth." Thessalonians 2:13

With all the experiments going on today, such as the hadron colliders built in Europe (CERN) and the United States, the antichrist is trying to build lies and spectacles for the eyes of man. He knows that, to conquer our hearts, first he needs to dazzle our senses and make us believe that he is, in fact, the Almighty and not

147

God. For that reason, experiments portrayed as noble today will transform, in time, into a tool of our own doom. Time travel, manipulation of matter and reality, even aliens, they will all be on the menu set forth in front of our eyes, and most of us will not know what to believe anymore at the sight of such 'wonders'.

"And he shall speak great words against the most High, and shall wear out the saints of the most High, and think to change times and laws: and they shall be given into his hand until a time and times and the dividing of time. But the judgment shall sit, and they shall take away his dominion, to consume and to destroy it unto the end." Daniel 7:25-26

We need to stay sharp and accept the truth behind all the things happening around us, right now! We need to stop gawking at their clever mouths, that speak so fast and so eloquently, and see beyond the frontline lies.

They say they want to discover the 'God Particle', as they cleverly call it, but these scientists have no idea that this is not the way to discover or to find God. One can only find God through the way of the heart, through prayer and devotion. You need to love and worship God to find him, because he is everywhere, but we have been blinded over the years. Scientism managed to convince us that nothing is wonderful in this world and that life itself, with all is wonders, was nothing but a fortunate accident.

With the passing of time, more and more lies will be pushed in front of our eyes and the enemy will play on the Flat Earth card, but only to distort the truth and intercept it with his own agenda. The gatekeepers (those who control mainstream information) are readily aware of the importance of the sort of information that reaches people's ears. Why let other sincere individuals disclose the truth in its rough form, if they can take it and twist to their own advantage? Sounds logical, right? Well, to them it is, and it's beneficial too. That is why you need to be careful about where you get your information from, because in your search for the truth, you might end up wandering on strange paths.

The Bible should always be your final source in your endeavor to find the truth. The earth is undoubtedly flat, and more and more evidence is being put on the table. People are starting to realize that they have been lied to for so many centuries, thus Scientism has prepared an arsenal of lies and false truths to bombard us with.

Chapter 10: Scientism and the alien agenda

And great earthquakes shall be in divers places, and famines, and pestilences; and fearful sights and great signs shall there be from heaven. Luke 21:11

Hollywood and Future events

Now, we'll talk about the role Hollywood played in history and how it influenced people's perception over the world and even science. We all like to go watch a movie every now and then, and now, with the current technology, we could easily install a home cinema, so we don't have to leave the comfort of our home anymore. Good for them! And I say this, because it's easier to program our thinking like this.

Some might see pure entertainment in a movie, but it's never like that! These so-called commercial productions aim at making loads of money, but, at the same time, they incorporate a subtle sort of programming. Just think of the logos some corporations have, (the globe) and you will quickly realize that we are being brainwashed, long before the film has even started.

This sort of subtle programming can be found throughout the films, from product placement to foreseeing events about to happen (announced or unannounced).

One perfect example would be the film, "A space odyssey", that appeared on the big screen, right before the Apollo missions landed the first man on the surface of the moon. The script of the film and the images filmed are probably 'too familiar' to those shot by Neil Armstrong and Buzz Aldrin. It's well known that the crew of the film never set foot on the moon, and yet, if you did not tell people that the film had been shot on earth, they could not tell the difference.

If you ask me, "A Space Odyssey" looks better on tape than the 'actual' moon footage. Another interesting fact was that the film was shot right before the alleged moon mission. I can't help but wonder, what was the actual purpose of that film? What were the directors and the people behind them trying to test people's reactions? Were they trying to induce a sort of social hysteria, designed to indoctrinate people in a much-needed trance for the things that followed?

One thing is clear. "A Space Odyssey" was a brilliant film, with a lot of money involved in the process, which meant that there was a great interest behind it. And, at the end of the day, this thing they called a movie provided NASA with all the necessary tools and materials to film another movie and call it 'The Real Moon Landing'. I was not there to see it with my own eyes, but it was clearly achievable. If they had managed to shoot the earth from a distance in "A Space Odyssey," they could certainly do it again.

What are we going to do, now that countless movies are depicting an alien invasion, right at our doorstep? Films, series... They all depict the aliens who are coming to say 'hi'. In some versions, these extraterrestrials are peaceful and friendly, while in some others, they are violent and ruthless, and people don't know what to believe anymore. In all scenarios though, we look like we're the nerds of the group, skinny and helpless, so much so that we don't stand a chance if a fight broke out.

The rhythm of these productions has intensified in the last two decades. Forget Star Trek, get ready for extermination, because it looks like that is on the menu. It's time for you to give up your freedoms and all your rights, if you still want to breathe tomorrow.

The truth is we have been lied to about space and what is out there, right from the beginning. Starting in the 1960's with "A Space Odyssey" and all the films that followed, they portrayed space as vast and always above us, from all points of view. The general belief installed in people's minds was that we should bow and feel humble, as we're too young and insignificant as a civilization, compared to what's supposed to be out there.

No proof behind their claims, and yet, we were made to believe that the universe is populated with countless species, older and more advanced than we will ever be. But I ask you this: What if the whole space thing is only an invention and the all-powerful aliens are nothing but the figure of our sick imaginations? Did you ever wonder how these Hollywood movies are created and how realistic they appear? I mean, if you would show one of these films (let's pick Prometheus, for example) to a person who has no idea of the alien agenda or anything else, I bet that they could not tell the difference between fiction and fact.

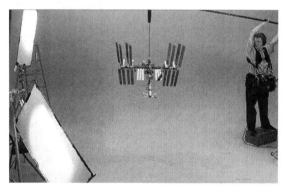 Nowadays, green screens and CGI can work wonders, with all these super computers we have, and the result can hardly be perceived as a lie. This is just one example that came to my mind, especially, because it included a different 'myth of creation'.

Ridley Scott shows us, at the beginning of his movie, how an 'alien' disintegrated into the waters of the world, and so, life spawned on Earth. Isn't this quite brilliant? I mean, a short scene at the beginning of the film, where the supposed creators of humanity are shown to be superior, both physically and mentally. In that movie, we are pushed towards one conclusion, that we are nothing but a degenerated progeny of a greater race, and not God's greatest achievement.

As a matter of fact, later in that movie, we can see how those aliens, who supposedly created us, were trying to eradicate us, but they failed, since the bug supposed to kill us went and killed them instead. Quite an irony, don't you think? We were saved by an accident. Even in the movies, we are a result of luck... It looks like the Copernican ideology and evolutionism are deeply rooted in Hollywood. The only difference is that, now, the survival does not belong to the fittest, but to the luckiest.

Satan's goal is to take control over the whole of humanity. And his only way of achieving this is through his minions on earth. His slaves, because I cannot call them otherwise.

Over the years, we have fought among each other, but we could never get on the same side, as there were individuals who spotted the lie and fought against it, till their last drop of blood. No internal enemy was frightening enough to convince everyone to lay down their freedoms and their dreams and to allow a single man or woman to rule over the whole world.

"In order to, one day, convince mankind of a threat substantial enough for them to hand global power over to one person, mankind had to first be convinced that space travel between planetary bodies is possible - regardless of the truth!" This was a classified statement from a top official, involved with the higher circles of government. He underlines perfectly this need for world domination or "New World Order", as Bush Sr. called it, and how an alien threat will be the best pretext for such a call from our leaders.

Stephen Hawking, the man who said that God is obsolete since we have science, kept repeating that we are in danger. His belief was that, if an alien civilization were to discover us, we would share the fate of the American Indians, when they came in contact with the Europeans, and by this, he meant extermination. A man who had no fear of God was so afraid of aliens, isn't this weird? I mean, I don't think he was afraid for himself, since he did not have that much left to live, but he was afraid for humanity, and kept underlining the idea of immediate danger and that we 'should do something'.

I wonder what that something might be, considering that he was a leading scientist, maybe the greatest scientist of 21st century, according to some, and a leading figure of Scientism, no doubt. According to their agenda, it is understandable that they keep pushing this sort of idea, that only united could we stand a feeble chance at survival against the malevolent aliens. Yes, together, which does not sound so bad, but under their rule and according to their rules, and this is nothing but disastrous.

Jesus taught us to love each other and to be united against evil, against Satan and all his lies, but we can clearly see how Scientism uses this fear and need for unity that mankind craves for, to guide us in their desired direction.

Richard Dawkins, a strong anti-God apostate, if I can call him that, during an interview with Ben Stein, he clearly accepted the idea of intelligent design, but he replaced God with some random alien civilization. He could hardly answer all the questions he was being asked, regarding the creation of life on earth, stating, "No one knows how it started, but we know what followed next!"

Isn't this pure ignorance? I ask you, because I basically started laughing, when I first heard his claims. To him and many others, the first moment does not really matter, as if everything following creation could happen anyway, if it were not for that first spark of life. When you look at them, they seem so certain in their beliefs, but with a few hard-core questions, you can feel their voice trembling. Why does that happen? Well, let me tell you why, because they don't hold all the answers. As a matter of fact, I don't think they hold any real answers at all, just baseless assumptions.

The alien creator was Dawkins' last idea, when he could not find any decent answer to all the questions he was being asked. And yet, even if he was telling the truth, and let's assume an advanced alien race created us, then, who created them? Maybe another even more advanced alien race? Then, who created those?

You see, we keep running on a never-ending spiral, because they can't find the final answer and accept God as our true Creator. Scientism tries to replace God in our lives, but they have nothing to replace him with, not at the same level at least, and there will always be gaps, empty spots in their theories that they could never explain.

In a way, it is funny how they are trying to explain the origins of life and mankind on this earth. People like Richard Dawkins, Neil deGrasse Tyson, and others are filling themselves with ridicule, even if they are not willing to admit it, and keep making false claims, probably hoping that if they insist long enough, people would buy the lie. The alien agenda is no different than any other type of propaganda, and they probably know that if they say the same thing repeatedly, eventually, something will get stuck in people's minds, especially if they target those who are too young to discern between truth and lies just yet.

We are being prepared for something that we're certainly not going to like nor accept easily. That's why they need to 'program' us, in a way, so that we become docile enough to accept even the most horrendous proposals, just for the sake of our physical safety. After all, we're meaningless, right? With no real power to do or achieve anything.

The Ancient Aliens Saga

Another 'beautiful' show, inspiring nonetheless, is one broadcasted on the History Channel, called "Ancient Aliens". I am sure you've all heard of it, and how they claim that the aliens did everything on this earth and we just stood and looked at them in awe. From the pyramids (both in Egypt and Central America) to other great stone buildings around the world, the show tries to convince us that we have been fathered by bearded aliens, who came from a planet, called Nibiru, somewhere hidden in our solar system.

Ancient Aliens: Extraterrestrial TV Show on the History Channel

Von Daniken, Giorgio Tsoukalos, and the rest of the hosts of this show, affirm strongly that man has been created by combining the DNA of a monkey with the DNA of the Annunaki (the so-called advanced aliens). We can see in the Bible that God created man in his own image and according to his liking, in order to rule over the whole earth and all the beasts living on it.

Then God said, "Let Us make man in Our image, according to Our likeness; and let them rule over the fish of the sea and over the birds of the sky and over the cattle and over all the earth, and over every creeping thing that creeps on the earth." God created man in His own image, in the image of God He created him; male and female He created them." Genesis 1:26-27

"This is the book of the generations of Adam. In the day when God created man, He made him in the likeness of God. He created them male and female, and He blessed them and named them Man in the day when they were created." Genesis 5:1-2

The most interesting part about the whole "Ancient Aliens" theory is the fact that the Annunaki supposedly created us as a slave race, to mine the gold for them, as it was too physically intensive for them. Isn't this beautiful? A so-called advanced race, capable of interstellar travel and creating new species by manipulating DNA, just could not find a better way of extracting gold from the ground. We could do it today with our current technology, and we're not as advanced as we might think, but those god-like aliens couldn't. Maybe they were environmentally aware and did not want to pollute the earth with cyanides or other related substances and that's why they went to the extent of creating a whole new species.

Carving depicting ancient Anunnaki

What upsets me the most about this theory is the fact that Von Daniken, Tsoukalos, nor their peers have any knowledge of history or ancient languages. They're just like politicians, who have no actual profession and are good only at spitting lies, right and left. The way these people are making connections between nonexistent leads is incredible, and the worst part is that they base their theory on some clay tablets that are thousands of years old, battered by wind and rain. No one even knows if the translation is even accurate, but that does not stop them from making all kinds of preposterous claims. When you look into their eyes, you can see they are convinced of their words, even if those words are actually empty of meaning.

This situation made me wonder. These people are not scientists, just some folks with a big mouth, who have no idea what they are talking about, so how are they doing it so effortlessly? Is this a different tactic of Scientism, to attack people with different means and on different levels, or they are just a bunch of clueless people, set on making a quick buck on the ignorance of the masses and their thirst for the sensational?

We know from the Bible that Abram and his descendants walked into Egypt and were enslaved by the pharaoh, right in the time the pyramids were built.

"And [God] said to Abram, Know positively that your descendants will be strangers dwelling as temporary residents in a land that is not theirs [Egypt], and they will be slaves there and will be afflicted and oppressed for 400 years." *Genesis 15:13*

The "Ancient Alien" paradigm insists that man could never build such magnificent constructions. Again, the same downsizing of humanity, where we are too little and too stupid to matter or accomplish anything significant. The only thing we could do was scramble through the ruins that the 'great aliens' left behind, when they left the Earth. Also, negating a strong Biblical case for fallen angels working with humans to advance society and bring technological wonders to the world.

The conclusion: we were left behind like waste or the second product of a greater process, and it was up to us to grow and multiply, just like God instructed us to do in Genesis. Don't you think this is a little bit ridiculous?

"And God blessed them, and God said unto them, "Grow and multiply, and fill the earth and subdue it, and have dominion over the fishes of the sea, and over the fowls of the air, and over all the beasts that move on the earth." Genesis 1:28

How the television and the alien agenda are distorting reality

Earlier, we mentioned predictive programming and how big companies are shaping our view towards reality. After all, we build our own reality, based on our senses and experiences, thus, they understood that if they could manipulate our perception, then, they could manipulate our beliefs and, eventually, our reality.

Corporate logos such as 'Universal' or 'Dream Works Studios' are more than suggestive. The globe, the moon hanging over the water, almost touching it, are elements that are supposed to crack into our subconsciousness. At times, these signals are contradictory, as if someone is trying to play with our mind, to test our limits and see how much we can take.

We might look at movies and cartoons, such as the Simpsons, Under the Dome, or the Signal, and perceive them as simple artistic renderings, but they are, in fact, a 'cute' and inoffensive way to prepare us for what's going to happen next. This sort of brainwashing technology worked perfectly thus far, since we are so in love with our television. They even call it 'television programming' upfront, and make it look like it's nothing, when, in fact, it is so intoxicating for any mind caught in its trap. We look, but we don't judge anymore. Aliens, monsters, apocalyptic scenarios... We just take it in, with a smile and scream for more.

"Judge not according to the appearance, but judge righteous judgment." John 7:24

Did you ever think why people are acting like this? Maybe, because they have been programmed from the day they opened their eyes and they know nothing else but this? If, 100 years ago, the idea of aliens was something new and taboo, now, it feels like it's a part of our lives and we can't wait to meet them (with all the dangers involved, of course).

Men in Black was another success, where the alien agenda is concerned, and Will Smith played that role wonderfully. Funny and engaging at the same time, the film portrays the Earth as an extraterrestrial hub, where countless species come and go, and the general population has no idea of what's going on. It feels, in a way, like a replica of the current reality we are living in. Everything is hidden and distorted and all we are being sold are fat lies.

As Hitler once said: "The bigger the lie, the more inclined people will be to believe it."

It is scary to know that mass murderers like Hitler have so much in common with the people who pose as our leaders today. With the same ideology, comes the same outcome, eventually, and thus, we need to be vigilant.

Now back to Men in Black. An interesting line caught my attention in the film, when Agent K (Tommy Lee Jones) tells Agent J (Will Smith):

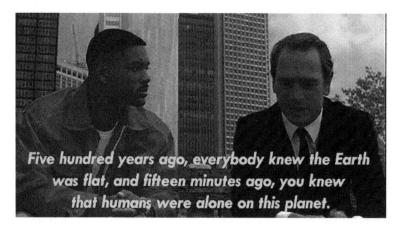

Five hundred years ago, everybody knew the Earth was flat, and fifteen minutes ago, you knew that humans were alone on this planet.

A person is smart. People are dumb, panicky, dangerous animals and you know it. 1500 years ago, everybody knew the Earth was the center of the universe, 500 years ago everybody knew the earth was flat, and fifteen minutes ago you knew that people were alone on this planet, imagine what you will know tomorrow!"

Isn't this beautiful? This is exactly the perception that the ruling class and Scientism has about us, the flock, the brainless masses, and that's why they are trying to lure us away from God and the universal truth. They mock our belief through movies and documentaries and, at the same time, they throw bits and pieces at us, to show us that they don't really care about our fate. They just want to rule, regardless of the means.

Another interesting fact, that is slightly separated from the 'official media' and the movies, is the phenomenon of alien abductions. Be it people, cows, or cats, we have all heard of instances, where the aliens scooped creatures from earth, teleported them to their mother ship, and performed all sort of experiments on them. No one can tell exactly what happened, since they all have foggy memories of strange looking creatures, that sometimes look friendly and sometimes not so friendly.

The purpose of these abductions is supposed to be the study of our reproductive system and of the cow's too, of course, probably because the poor super advanced aliens can't have sex anymore, and they need us to teach them. It would be ludicrous to think that a species so advanced (able to create ships that defy the laws of physics and gravity) would need us in order to perpetuate their species (let's say they have a genetic malfunction, the way some people claimed).

Right now, we are being assaulted on all sides by this Alien propaganda. Movies, abductions, crop circles, documentaries, that there are people who are scared of them and people who are eager to meet them. It all looks like mayhem that's right at our doorstep and we know nothing about it, just yet.

Scientism and its propaganda are trying to make us look weak in the face of danger, especially when talking about an alien threat. By listening to all these stories that have been propagated so far, we can observe how we can easily be manipulated by these so-called grays or what other skin colors they might be. They are able to turn us into stone and play with our bodies as they like, and there is nothing we can do to prevent it from happening. The best we can do is watch and wait to see if they are going to kill us in the end.

These are nothing but demonic attacks, and the parallels are striking when you look into possession cases. The same paranormal activity is happening, so it's clear when you have the Bible as your authority, that you can see this as a deception of the enemy. In order for the world to accept such fantasies, of these beings travelling from other planets, a scientific worldview must be put in place to give the reality of such life occurring in the first place, in some distant galaxy. While much has been said about various lies in Scientism, it's important to understand that it also prepares humanity for what's to come.

How it all began

The Copernican revolution sits at the core of the alien life paradigm, whereas the universe is infinite, and after the Big Bang, stars and planets were created. If the accident of life happened on earth, then, it could happen elsewhere in the universe, at least a couple of times. After all, we are told that we are not so special, just a speck of dust in the universe, and there's a lot of dust out there.

You must understand how the alien agenda works. We never heard about aliens until the 20th century, at least not so broadly, and that's because it would have sounded like an absurdity. People knew from the Bible that God had created the earth, all the animals and plants on it, and then, He created Adam and Eve, and that was it. The Bible does not talk about other 'earths' or 'super earths', as they are calling them these days, let alone about other 'alien' species. Therefore, humanity had to be introduced, slowly but gradually, to the concept of the endless universe and how life was not created but evolved from nothing.

This way, aliens would come to life. They were not born on distant planets and did not evolve from some lizard or something, but they were rather born in the mind of Satan, who was determined to turn God's order and the world upside down. As soon as the earth started spinning, in 'people's perception', obviously, and the evolution theory was set on track, then, this new ideology could be set in motion. And it was easy to achieve. All Scientism needed to do was to dazzle people's senses and convince them that they have seen something in the sky. After all, these intelligent beings need humanity to fall for the deception. In ancient times, they referred to these demons as gods, but, through a clever Scientism endgame, they now see them as intelligent, evolved species from another planet.

The "Goldilocks Zone" is another scientific invention, meaning that planets that orbit in that area are habitable. And yes, of course, each star has such a zone around it. It makes me laugh. With so many variables and details necessary for life, I believe these people are out of their minds to think that they will find the same conditions we have on another 'planet'. But as we have learned, the Earth is not a 'planet.'

The thing is, their lies have started to reach the edge of the cliff and, for that reason, they have nowhere else to go. This is the time for them to win over our hearts or die. Scientism knows it has limited time, as anything else that has ever existed on this earth. So now, they are playing the alien card, in their attempt to break us completely from God. They want to replace God with another entity, supposedly as powerful as God, but, nonetheless, a lot more powerful than we are.

Scientism claims that the earth and the solar system are of a medium age, thus we are mediocre in this aspect, too. With a 13-billion-year-old universe and a 4,5 billion year old earth, we're 1/3 of that age, therefore, there could be other aliens out there, older and more advanced than we are… or not.

Scientists realized the lie they were perpetuating, and they realized that they could not go on forever with it, and they did not have to look out there through the millions and billions of stars and galaxies. No! All they had to do was put a drop of water under the microscope and wonder at the complexity of earth's ecosystem at the smallest level.

Right now, we have no idea how many creatures live here with us. We think we caught a few and named them, but the vast majority is still unknown, and from the smallest to the biggest, each fills a specific role that makes the world go on. Scientists did not even grasp the complexity of God's creation, but the signs of an intelligent design are there, and they are visible, both to the naked eye and to the microscope.

As Richard Dawkins said, 'there might be an intelligent design behind humanity from some place in the universe' in the interview with Ben Sterns for the documentary Expelled: No Intelligence Allowed. Resulting from this, another belief has started to grow among the adepts of Scientism, and the funny fact is that it simply copies the Bible. Now, there are the adepts of the alien creator, who are waiting for the second coming of their supposed God. Instead of waiting for Christ's second coming, people are waiting for some 'alien' that they had never seen or really heard of.

Isn't this lunacy? Have we lost our sense of judgment completely? How come people reject God, our creator, and rejoice at the thought of some alien creature they no idea existed in the first place? Has scientism managed to brainwash us to this extent? It looks like they managed to reach a great number of people, mainly, because they hold the mainstream media and control everything written in textbooks.

A recent event, where a teacher in the United States wanted to teach creationism and intelligent design in school, was viciously attacked and was threatened with the loss of his job because of his choice. It's clear that people who dare to speak the truth will be censored and pushed to a dark corner, until people will hopefully forget about them, but this is not reason enough for us to stop fighting.

The alien-demigod is obviously the current narrative. And I believe the writing is on the wall. The future we're expecting is going to show us an event, Independence Day style, a great lie, dressed in a 'purple' coat, that will aim at making people fall on their knees and beg for mercy, and the targets are those who still believe in God.

Maybe the aliens will simply provide the reason for those in power to hide behind the curtains and wipe humanity out, or maybe they will pretend to be our benefactors and congratulate us for our achievement, while offering to help us reach new heights. The dices have not been rolled out just yet, it's clear to me, and Scientism is still making plans, calculating, and trying to find the best scenario for humanity. The aliens could probably come with the model for 'global unity' and tell us. 'look what we achieved with one world government, you could do the same'.

Another case, where the aliens show up at our doorstep, they will probably want to 'speak' to the ruler of the world, and we will be forced to 'unite' and give them that person to talk to. You know, it is always easier to strike a deal with one individual than to convince a group.

In Star Trek, the earth is portrayed as a united conglomeration of peoples, where the notion of distinct country has long since disappeared from people's minds. Everything is beautiful in the movie, people are happy and smiling, and there are even instances and hints where the characters mock the old organization of the world, claiming that they could not understand how people could live with borders and why they did not create that world government sooner, because it's so good and awesome... Yeah, right! (another example of preemptive programming).

We humans are not that hard to impress, especially when talking about crucial aspects of our lives, such as disease eradication, clean energy, and longer lifespans (maybe immortality). We have been craving immortality for ages, thus, creating myths such as the Fountain of Youth or the Holy Grail. These aliens, who will portray themselves as our creators, will probably aim to satisfy our deepest desires, in order to win us over, and then, the big surprise will unfold. With our eyes dazzled from all the 'goodies' we received from them and our minds confused, we will not flinch in saying 'yes'... at least, that's what they think.

Without even knowing what is going on, we will find ourselves in the middle of a 'galactic war' and, under the pressure of time, we will be forced to pick sides. The good aliens (our creators) will soon pose as victims, mentioning a ferocious enemy heading our way, and how they need our help to defeat it.

A red flag should pop up in people minds immediately, don't you think? We aren't even able to cure cancer or clean up the Earth, and yet, we are asked to help an obviously superior alien race fight a 'bad alien', who is even stronger than they are. How are we supposed to do anything, since we're nothing but a backwater civilization with lousy technology? Things do not add up here, but this will not stop the alien agenda from playing this card, and it will do it, because there is a catch in this, and the lie is absolutely demonic.

"Why do the heathen rage, and the people imagine a vain thing? The kings of the earth set themselves, and the rulers take counsel together, against the LORD, and against his anointed, saying, Let us break their bands asunder, and cast away their cords from us.

He that sitteth in the heavens shall laugh: the Lord shall have them in derision. Then shall he speak unto them in his wrath, and vex them in his sore displeasure. Yet have I set my king upon my holy hill of Zion." Psalm 2:1-6

The so-called enemy we are supposed to fight against is not really an alien, or our enemy for that matter, but the son of God, who will come to earth for the second time on judgment day. Satan will play with mankind, hoping that God will not unleash his wrath, seeing his children ready to face him. The devil plays on God's love for humanity, thinking that he would win against the Almighty this way, but he is spreading only false hope and lies, able only to deceive the human mind, as they have no effect against God. Humanity will be deceived into thinking that this threat is a hostile alien invasion and will work with Satan to try and defeat God. Such madness. But when the world has been programmed to fight for its survival, with the aid of some benevolent beings from other worlds, it will be seen as the right action to take. It's sad, when you actually think of the reality that only destruction will be brought upon those who do not submit to the true Creator.

Pride goeth before destruction, and a haughty spirit before a fall. Proverbs 16:18

Satan managed to trick Adam and Eve, back in the garden of Eden, disguised as a snake and whispering lies into the woman's ears. The dreams of greatness and power and the vanity of being God-like have never vanished entirely from people's hearts, and that's exactly what Satan will exploit now, as we get closer to the end of times.

The second phase of Satan's deceptive plan has already been put in place, in the last half millennium, but more insistently in the last couple of decades.

Now, we hear from all directions that we might actually be Martians. Yeah, you heard it right, it looks like somewhere in the last few billions years, some sort of impact happened and a piece of rock was thrown into space and ended up landing on earth and that's how you and I came into being, eventually, of course, after millions of years of evolution and after a monkey just got sick of walking on four legs and climbing through trees and decided it was time for a change.

The same scientists who come up with these preposterous ideas and claim that they have better judgment, because they are 'men/women of science', laugh at the thought that we might have been created, by an intelligent God, who knew exactly what he was creating and left nothing to chance.

Scientism knows not the way of the truth, and every time someone asks these big mouth scientists if they have any argument against Genesis or Adam and Eve, they just swallow their words and change the subject. Just watch one video interview and notice the long pauses in their speech, every time they are asked to contradict the creation story from Genesis. This happens, because they have no idea what to say. They are boldly against the Bible, but they cannot provide any real alternative, therefore, they come up with all sorts of crazy ideas: descendants of Martians, we're the result of fallen comets, or we just appeared out of nothing.

No real proof exists out there to prove that we evolved from monkeys or from alien rocks fallen from the sky. A bone or two they find in the African savanna proves absolutely nothing. Maybe that something lived around the place, at a certain point in time, and now, it's dead.

Bill Nye, a fervent supporter of the alien agenda, calls the belief in creation and genesis as a betrayal of the intellect, saying that there is no other proof than the Word of God, written in the Holy Bible. But does he have any proof that we are derived from Martians or from organisms that once lived on mars, God knows how long ago? Not Really! And yet, he strongly believes that we are the descendants of some aliens, and, in his eyes, that is definitely not a betrayal of the intellect.

That is CRAZY! Absolutely crazy, because he applies different judgments to two similar situations, and, in the case of Adam and Eve, we have the Word of God, let's not forget that.

But it's okay! Every time we ask for proof, something to show us that their theories and assumptions are correct, they throw the same old lie at us... "well, we can't do this right now, but it's a work in progress, and as soon as we get something, we'll let you know!" Aha, right. That work in progress will never end, because there is no work and no progress in the first place, just a big, fat lie that's meant to keep us in the dark and under their rule.

It's simple folks, the spacecrafts they are talking about, those that are supposedly digging for the truth as we speak, do not exist. All those rovers that supposedly wander on the surface of mars, the probes sent into the solar system for research purposes, they are just pictures and CGI, made up by highly intelligent people, no doubt, but people who are hiding a tenebrous agenda.

The UFO phenomenon has developed into a public frenzy, during the past few decades, and yet, at first no government or agency admitted that such things existed. They played the blind card up to a point, probably to test the waters and see what people's reaction will be in the end. They needed to prepare their strategy, according to people's reactions. They always act like this, and when they finally come out, everything fits like a glove.

That is the case with NASA astronauts, like Mitchell and even Aldrin, who, at some point, openly admitted that they have seen UFO's out there. They were clearly under deep security clearance and they still talked, as if they were recalling their last weekend spent with their families. Of course, no penalty followed, despite the general rule in these sorts of situations, and this makes me believe that these were planned events, carefully planted in people's minds.

After all, the famous Apollo astronauts were talking now, and since everyone 'knew' they had landed and walked on the moon, they could not lie about the alien sighting... Or could they?

The leaks have undoubtedly been planned, and it feels like a cat and mouse game, where, at a certain point, they stop plotting and 'allow' us to catch them. If the disclosure were real, then Aldrin and all the others would have rotted in jail for the rest of their lives. Just look at what happened to Edward Snowden, who did some real uncovering and had to flee the country, and now, the poor man has the CIA, NSA, FBI, and any other agency I can think of on his back. Why? Because he was not working with them and wanted the people to know the real truth and not the fabricated one.

Soon, they will come to us with a grand disclosure and a bunch of reasons as to why they did not tell us about the alien presence in the first place. Of course, those reasons regarded our own well-being, no doubt. And many people are going to fall for this lie, unfortunately, and the Bible says exactly how it is going to happen.

"And then shall that Wicked be revealed, whom the Lord shall consume with the spirit of his mouth, and shall destroy with the brightness of his coming: Even him, whose coming is after the working of Satan with all power and signs and lying wonders, And with all deceivableness of unrighteousness in them that perish; because they received not the love of the truth, that they might be

saved. And for this cause God shall send them strong delusion, that they should believe a lie: That they all might be damned who believed not the truth, but had pleasure in unrighteousness.

But we are bound to give thanks always to God for you, brethren beloved of the Lord, because God hath from the beginning chosen you to salvation through sanctification of the Spirit and belief of the truth: Whereunto he called you by our gospel, to the obtaining of the glory of our Lord Jesus Christ. Therefore, brethren, stand fast, and hold the traditions which ye have been taught, whether by word, or our epistle." 2 Thessalonians 8-15

If you look around you with a careful eye, you can see that we are surrounded by lies and illusions right now. We are focused on the 'marketing' of everything and cast aside the real value of things and people. What's on the outside is the only thing that matters, while the essence of things is regarded as something inessential.

The deception is in training right now, but, at the end of days, we will see the greatest illusions humanity has ever seen in its history and they will be shrouding the antichrist, who will pose as the holiest of them all, with all signs and wonders, which the entire world will adore; the exact opposite of Jesus' entrance in Jerusalem.

Chapter 11: Scientism and the future

And that no man might buy or sell, save he that had the mark, or the name of the beast, or the number of his name. Rev 13:17

C. S. Lewis said: "I dread government in the name of science, that's how tyrannies come in!"

This can be considered as an alarming conclusion, because he clearly understood how people could use something apparently 'objective' and truth-based, such as science and turn it into a tool of propaganda and tyranny.

It is also dangerous to create an ideology, where the only way to learn the truths about the world is through the science controlled by a handful of people. If we reach a point, where we discard everything else deemed as un-scientific, and we throw it away, without even analyzing the possibility that it might be true, then we have taken on a dark path.

Imagine so much power, in the hands of just a few people, imagine the temptation for corruption. We all know from history how people reacted when they knew that they were not accountable for their actions. Politicians and rulers of all sorts changed the face of the earth with their crimes and atrocities.

The Bible tells us how God is the ultimate judge for all humanity and how we will be held accountable for our sins on Judgment Day. Every Christian knows this for a fact, and yet, the Scientism movement is trying to convince us otherwise. According to their ideology, with our flesh, dies everything else, and we vanish from history, thus, no matter what we do here, it will fade away, anyway.

Therefore, according to their philosophy, we're free to do whatever we like, if we can get away with it in this life.

We're bound to talk about the future in this chapter, but thinking about it, I must go back in the past and make the connection between 'end game' theory, as I like to call it, and the social movements that emerged from Scientism.

Communism as a direct result of Scientism and evolutionism was the cause for tens of millions of victims, from China to Eastern Europe, and even Central and South America. Millions of souls perished from this world in an unjust manner, only because the leaders of those communist parties believe the world began and will end with them. Right now, it might seem ludicrous and distant when thinking about it, but, back then, millions died and billions of people suffered, because some people denied God and posed themselves as Gods.

Now let's return to today's Scientism. Indeed, it did not die, but it's not like what it used to be. Rather, it changed its coat and tried different techniques, even if the core ideas are the same.

They still claim they know what is best for us, and that only they should decide what should happen to humanity and to each one of us in the future.

A 'Soft Dictatorship', I call this new agenda of theirs. And I see it as 'soft' only for the time being, because only God knows what it will transform into eventually. Our morals and beliefs are at stake right now, and our way of life too, because, little by little, they will attempt at taking over everything.

Scientism, and the way in which they began using technology to control us, is very dangerous. We might not know it now, because we see it as a game, but in the end, we will become the slaves, while they will turn into our masters. I look around and see how people are oblivious to the danger, although it is right there in front of them. I guess this happens, because they learned our weaknesses and know exactly what cards to play at the right time.

At first, they turn everything into a game, because we love our entertainment so much. They are the ones who snuck that love under our skin at first, and now, they are exploiting their investment.

Their subterfuge is rather brilliant. They made us think that we want the things they're throwing at us. We don't need them, and yet, we bask in this sea of ignorance, we give up our freedom and intimacy to gain what? Safety?

The science behind all this has nothing good in it, their intention is evil and wicked, and when we wake up one day as prisoners inside our own homes, praying to God, we should remember why we gave up and for what?

Destroying our privacy and our mental processes are only some of the means used to brainwash and control us, and we see some extraordinary things being displayed in front of our eyes.

With the decoding of the DNA and the sequencing of genes, people started believing that we had reached the stage of gods now, and that we could manipulate life, according to our interests. After the 1990's, we could see a rampant growth in gene technology manipulation and how people began experimenting at first with plants and animals, and then, they quickly turned their sights on the human race.

Various companies and corporations started creating and patenting new species for commercial profit. The Double Helix (DNA) is the cornerstone of all creation. These are the instructions God gave every cell and every living being, so it can function properly, and now, they are playing with God's creation.

No wonder we are seeing more and more sick people today, more and more sick animals. What could be the cause for all this? I'd say it all happened because people dared to interfere with God's creation. We've reached a point where we don't believe divine creation is perfect anymore and we see fit to perfect it. Isn't this absolutely ludicrous? 'Scientists' started believing that they we above God and that they can improve or completely change God's creation.

Wouldn't it be brilliant for you to be able to opt for a 6-foot, blonde-haired, genius baby? Who would not want that? But then, there comes the macabre side of this game. God gave us free will in this world and a chance for everyone to enjoy life, according to their efforts. Poor people could have brilliant children and rich folks could have dumb offspring, as well. This situation kind of equalized the world and gave everyone a chance.

With the idea of eugenics, Scientism proposes a completely new paradigm for this world, where the rich become superhumans, and the rest of us are thrown somewhere in a dark corner to die and rot, since we will become inferior to them.

As I said, the idea of the 'superhuman' is not new. German fascists kept talking about the Aryan Race, another occult 'creation', but unfortunately for them, they did not possess the tools to create such a human. That did not stop them from conducting all kinds horrible experiments on people and even children.

I say we should not go back to that point, where a group of people regards another group as mere animals, worthy of being slaughtered with no mercy.

The creation of the superhuman who would be able to breathe underwater, and God knows what else, has been the main purpose of the Scientism movement. Since the human being is God's ultimate creation, by modifying it and creating a 'better' version in their eyes and the eyes of the world, they probably think they will have the last proof they need, in order to prove that God does not exist.

Right now, the word on every scientist's lips, who are working with genetics and DNA, is CRISPR, and how miraculous this technology can be in gene manipulation and disease treatment. It sounds too good to be true and I am afraid this is just another Trojan horse, used to accomplish their dirty agenda. It appears that CRISPR offers scientists the opportunity to tinker with the software of life, modify it and change it in ways we, the regular folk, could not even imagine.

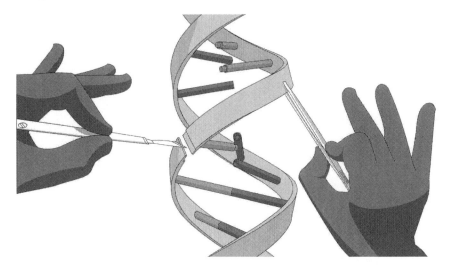

Personally, I really don't understand their excitement on this matter, because they act like they finally managed to grasp the hand of God, when, in fact, they are about to open Pandora's box.

For thousands of years, humans managed to breed horses and other animals for their desires almost as nature does, and no tragedy happened in the process. Now, with CRISPR, people can design the animals in a lab, and the same principle applies to humans… a really frightening perspective. With the help of this new technology, gene editing has become so easy, you could compare it with a word processor.

For better or worse, every living creature on earth will soon be affected by our capacity to reprogram the software of life. We might not know it yet, but soon, we might not have a single species that's the same as its ancestors living 100 years ago, because now, we'll be talking about gene contamination.

The genome is not like a concrete block, and during the reproductive process, genes get mixed up, so a new life is born. With gene editing and reformation, completely new genes will appear in the equation, transforming the game from the ground up. The new mixture of genes will basically erase the old, natural version of animals and plants, and create new mutants, with probably disastrous effects.

What frightens me the most is the fact that scientists are all excited about their new discovery, but they have no idea of the true effects this technology will have. It like a child's play with trial and error, until we hopefully learn how things work. We're playing with the world and with ourselves and we are doing it with a big smile on our faces.

I often wonder if people have lost their minds. I am talking about those members of Scientism, those scientists who literally play God and feel good about it, and most probably don't feel any responsibility towards humankind when they commit such atrocities. They want us to believe that they are intelligent, probably an elite category of society, and yet they act in a brainwashed manner, endangering our future on this world.

God gave us the earth to guard and protect, not to exploit it, as if it were our exclusive property. We were created last, because God wanted us to witness his power, beauty, and perfection of his creation. Are we seeing it anymore these days? I don't believe so, since Scientism keeps shouting loud and high that everything needs improvement, everything needs to be changed, because, in our sick eyes, nothing is how it's supposed to be anymore. This is the effect of an overgrown ego that overshadows our common sense.

Now, let's talk about the "Human Genome Project", which aimed at building the large plant and animal genomes. Let me make it clear for you, the genetics agenda of Scientism is building 'humans' who present better genetic features such as intelligence and athletics and market it as a consumer-based evolution of choice. In simple words, they are trying to turn God's creation, the human being, into a consumer product.

Countless people have opposed this idea, because it is both ungodly and unethical, and yet, the people who promote gene editing in humans keep on developing their 'products', as if they're blind and deaf to everything happening around them. Simply put, they don't care that people do not desire this abomination to take place, because they know there will be people (wealthy people, of course) who will buy into it just, so they can be ahead of everyone else, but they don't know what they are getting into.

"Once the technology is proven safe," as the scientists behind this project put it, we should just jump at it and embrace this new era, where we can buy our virtues with paper dollars. Earning your place in God's eyes seems too hard for them, therefore, they want to use this subterfuge, where you can cheat your fate in the same way the serpent cheated Adam and Eve in the garden of Eden.

We return again to the same paradigm where God's creation tries to 'defeat' God himself by changing and altering His creation. Satan has worked throughout millennia to corrupt us and it looks like he reached the pinnacle of his efforts, but we must not give up; we must fight back for what is right and true.

There was a talk about limits and boundaries, even this new technology could not avoid but all this is just in principle. There are no walls or fences that could stop them from reaching complete madness with their gene editing. The consensus within scientism is that we should go too far and test the limits, because they think this is the only way we could finally prove we reached the state of gods!

For you to understand that they're serious about their agenda, in January 2009, Obama nominated John Holdren as Chief Science Advisor. This man has previously proposed the creation of a 'Planetary Regime" to determine the "Optimum population for the world and for each individual region."

Recent headlines like these are where things are heading with this scientific dictatorship.

- The EPA is accused of withholding important scientific data from Congress.

- An Indiana Physics professor was censored for discussing intelligent design in class.

- College cancels class on evolution debate after 'Free thought' group threatens disruption.

There are just a few examples to show you where we are heading currently, with this new world religion, called Scientism. They keep blaming the inquisition and call for other horrors caused by Christianity in the past, but when you see headlines such as "Arrest of climate change deniers" really makes my body shiver, because it looks like we're going up on the terror ladder. When you control the world, you control the narrative, and clearly, Scientism has taken hold firmly. You are never to question them nor the direction they may take you in.

Something that used to be objective and had the purpose of making people's lives better has turned into a dictatorship. Right now, democracy is on the verge of being replaced by something we neither recognize nor want in our lives, and yet, it keeps being shoved down our throats against our will. Scientism is an evil agenda, religion, and theory that every man and woman on this earth should be aware of.

Another aspect that should make us jump out of our chairs is their obsession with identifying every single one of us, so they can have full control over the world. As mentioned previously, with the case of social media and surveillance cameras all over the western world, they are trying to get into your life, your home, and eventually, into your soul. The lack of development is, unfortunately, a setback for these power-hungry moguls, as in parts of the world such as Africa and Asia, almost two billion people live without an ID card or passport. Therefore, they cannot reach those people... yet.

For that reason, the World Bank is urging governments around to the world to find a 'cost-effective' method to bring those 'unidentified' people to civilization. No one asked those people if they wanted IDs or food, and I guess no one will ever ask them.

What turns the rage on inside me is the way in which these crooked banksters are presenting their evil agenda. They put on, as if those people without IDs are denied essential services, such as a loan probably?

You're wrong if you thought this was only a concept. On a smaller scale, the tagging process has already started, where in collaboration with the United Nations High Commissioner for Refugees, biometric ID cards have been issued for refugee camps in Thailand, South Sudan, and elsewhere.

It's happening people, right under our eyes, and what do we do? I knew they've always dressed their dark intentions in shining coats, but we should see beyond the smoke screen; the truth is there.

"Let no man deceive himself if any man among you seen to be wise in the world made him become a fool that he may be wise, for this wisdom of the world is foolishness with God." 1 Corinthians 3:18-21

We're living through times now, where people are starting to believe they are the masters of the world. The only ones who hold the absolute truth, therefore, they should become the ones deciding for everyone else. If they believe we should obey them, then, that's what they are going to try to achieve.

One of the best ways in which full control can be achieved is through dismantling intimacy and the idea that individuals have the right to a private life. Under the threat of global terrorism (whatever that might be) and other threats that we have not heard of just yet, they're going to push an agenda, where every one of us will be chipped under the skin and as the revelation says, no man or woman will be able to buy or sell things, unless they wear the mark of the beast.

"And all the world wondered after the beast." Revelation 13:3

We've seen this done already with animals, so they can't get lost anymore, and now they're trying to do the same thing with children. There are countries around the world like in Scandinavia where parents are chipping their child, but they have no idea what they are getting those poor little souls into.

It drives me crazy when I see those 'funny' commercials, where smiling, clueless people are pushing this propaganda onto us. "It's safe; it's for your own good," I keep hearing, yeah right! It's good, but not for us, not in the long run, as they are trying to get us to a point where they can simply starve us to death, if they wish … Whole populations, just so they can meet their new world order agenda.

Just try to imagine a world, where there is no cash anymore, and your access to food and water can be restricted with a simple push of a button. You're standing in front of the store, with your chip turned off, and all you keep hearing is that you have been denied. This image might look scary, but it's not so far from the truth these Scientism adepts are thinking of right now.

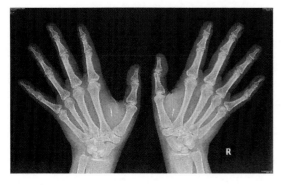

In order to convince us that chipping is good for us, they keep exploiting our 'currency' and how unbearable it is to carry your cash with you, as if a few banknotes could weigh a hundred pounds or something. Wow, it is so easy, so comfortable to just slide your hand in front of their machines and all you want is yours, but what if that stops working one day? What then? Frankly, I am a little bit skeptic about the credit cards and everything related to them right now, and I don't want to reach the point where I can't even hold a piece of plastic in my hand… It's scary! What are we supposed to do? Keep our hands inside our empty pockets?

Their ultimate dream is to possess the power to erase people from the world, simply and effectively. In the end, you'll only be a number for them, a number that can be deleted from the system, and then, let's see how you can survive without anything. All the resources will be in their hands and the rest of us will be at their mercy… if they'll have any of that.

"And he had power to give life unto the image of the beast, that the image of the beast should both speak, and cause that as many as would not worship the image of the beast should be killed. And he causeth all, both small and great, rich and poor, free and bond, to receive a mark in their right hand, or in their foreheads: And that no man might buy or sell, save he that had the mark, or the name of the beast, or the number of his name. Here is wisdom. Let him that hath understanding count the number of the beast: for it is the number of a man; and his number is Six hundred threescore and six." Revelation 13:15-18

The world's science and technology agenda is leading us to such a time as this.

The person, the soul, does not matter to them. We're just meat and bones, and that's why they are struggling so much to convince us of that idea, that we're nothing of importance, really, just creatures that evolved accidentally, living on a regular planet, orbiting a not-so-special star, somewhere in the backwaters of a random galaxy.

The Chinese scientists say that they are going to start human gene manipulation, and even if they state that they don't really understand the consequences involved in the process, it does not look like they are scared in any way of this. Their attitude is fairly understandable, since the Chinese Communist Party is persecuting Christians in China, as we speak. From a moral and religious point of view, this Scientism driven society is at the stage of the Roman Empire in the 1st century AD.

This sort of social cocktail, where people matter less and the Government can vote for genocide at any moment of the day is the perfect playground for people who have no fear of God. This is the perfect place for them to experiment and try new abominable things.

It is, indeed, an 'oligarchic paradise', and this is probably the main reason why our corporations love this system, where there is no justice for the poor and no possibility for redemption.

The starting point of this new agenda is somewhat mild, as the people involved in the phenomenon are talking about body regeneration and growing body parts, such as limbs or full organs, to replace the missing or damaged ones. Keep in mind though, that it's just the beginning of the end, because after they grow a heart, let's say, they're planning on growing a full human body around it.

I can't stop wondering what these creatures will look like? How will they behave? We know from Genesis that God gave us his breath for us to come alive, and that our soul is our treasure and the thing that makes us whole.

Men will never be able to create a soul, because it is impossible for us to do such things, regardless of how smart we think we are or how great our technology is. The soul is divine, eternal, and it can only come from God. It looks like Scientism is ready to create an army of zombies, mindless, soulless creatures, probably designed to eventually replace us.

The elite does not need a crowd that's able to think and judge. They don't need that hassle, but only a couple of docile hands, ready to do their bidding and dirty work for them. They can't put this idea up front, not yet, so that's why they're using Scientism for the job. This fake science is used like a battering ram against our gates, because they're planning to get it done, one way or another.

There are still feeble cases, where people who are a part of the movement are speaking 'the truth', such as Climate Scientist James Lovelock who said: "It may be necessary to put democracy on hold for a while," for the sake of saving the environment, no doubt!

These are nothing but satanic thoughts, because Satan cannot accept democracy or free will. He wants to dominate us by force and subterfuge.

Now, looking back at the climate change 'religion' and how this changing climate can change our future. I keep hearing all over the media that we must do something to save the Earth and how tens of thousands of scientists (climate scientists or not) agree that the stuff is real and how we are killing our world. It makes me laugh and cry at the same time. Indeed, we have been doing some damage in the past 200 years, at least, starting with the industrial revolution, and countless species have gone extinct because of us.

Biologist Daniel Lieberman from Harvard University reached a stunning conclusion: "We have evolved to need coercion". To him and people like him, humanity has grown defective, and now, we need their intervention in order to restore us to our 'normal' path.

I wonder what that path might be, because it looks to me that now Scientism started believing that all of God's creation is defective and needs urgent changing. All these outrageous ideas started popping up in the last few decades and they all come at once to overwhelm us. The tactic is rather simple, for everyone who cares to look at it. They first create the boogeyman, the enemy, the danger, and then they throw all sorts of crazy solutions at us, hoping we would accept at least one eventually, just for the sake of being saved from the face of danger.

I guess people will eventually breathe carbon instead of oxygen, so we can reduce global warming or however it's being called these days. They keep changing the names of these phenomena. We first had global warming and when they saw that the earth was not warming anymore, they changed it to climate change... Quite convenient.

The Bible clearly teaches us that weather will change around the world, as we move into the end times, and having a Big Bang cosmology presented and taught to the masses can hide more truth of the true creator of creation.

What does the Bible teach about weather patterns in the end times that the world could be hiding with the "Climate Change" deception?

And as he sat upon the mount of Olives, the disciples came unto him privately, saying, Tell us, when shall these things be? and what shall be the sign of thy coming, and of the end of the world? And Jesus answered and said unto them, Take heed that no man deceive you. For many shall come in my name, saying, I am Christ; and shall deceive many. And ye shall hear of wars and rumours of wars: see that ye be not troubled: for all these things must come to pass, but the end is not yet. For nation shall rise against nation, and kingdom against kingdom: and there shall be famines, and pestilences, and earthquakes, in divers places. All these are the beginning of sorrows. Matthew 24:3-31

He hath made the earth by his power, He hath established the world by his wisdom, And hath stretched out the heavens by his discretion. When he uttereth his voice, there is a multitude of waters in the heavens, And he causeth the vapours to ascend from the ends of the earth; He maketh lightnings with rain, And bringeth forth the wind out of his treasures. Jeremiah 10:12–13

As we see in the Bible, God is in charge of the weather and all people, good and evil, are dependent on His provision. (Mathew 5:45-46) In an indirect way, all-natural disasters are God's judgement, as part of the fallen world. After the first man sinned, God cursed the ground (Genesis 3:17) and subjected the whole of creation to His frustration. (Romans 8:20-22) Therefore, Jesus warned us that, as long we are in this world, we will have tribulation. (John 16:33) Nevertheless, God has not abandoned us to random natural disasters, and He can and does use these for His purposes, even if it is just to remind us of our fragility and mortality, or to give the opportunity for Christians to show whether they really do love those who are suffering, as well as being witnesses to the fact that God has a better future for all who repent of their sins and put their trust in Christ, the Creator and Saviour.

Scientism has convinced the entire world that if we just reduce our carbon footprint, we can reverse all the damage that has been done. We can slow down the floods, earthquakes, hailstorms, and other natural disasters, but this is all a lie. "Global Warming" never worked out, so they conveniently changed it to "Climate Change," yet there is very little science backing it. Actually, the founder of The Weather Channel, John Coleman, was best known for championing skepticism about the human role in climate change and he wrote on his blog in December 2017, "There is no significant, man-made global warming at this time, there has not been any in the past and there is no reason to fear any in the future."

Even with many scientists coming forward with evidence refuting the man-made climate change agenda, the world will press on, trying to convince mankind of the impending dangers that face everyone, unless we fall in line with Scientism and the future direction we all need to take, according to the top officials and the elite.

Nick Bostrom, an Oxford University professor stated: "Current humanity need not be the end point of evolution."

According to this idea, we should be transforming into something else, but what? When God created us, he made in his image and according to his liking, therefore, we were, in fact, the ambassadors for God on earth. I don't know if we were created perfect, but we were definitely the best we could be. God created us like this, because he saw in us the right shape and the right measures.

Now, it looks like we need to step up to the next level and become something else. Being humans is not enough anymore, for some people, because they think that most of us will be left 'behind'.

It's ludicrous to think that we're supposed to be this uniform mass, where no individual can be distinguished from the others. I guess that scientists think we should be like the chicken in a poultry farm, all white and all fat. With the fat part, I think they already started a long time ago, but that's a discussion for another day.

Professor of Practical Ethics Julian Savulescu, from Oxford University said, "Genetically enhance humans or face extinction."

From reading the Bible, we can see how humans have lived on earth for thousands of years, in perfect harmony with nature, and even if we did not have advanced medicine or antibiotics, we still managed to survive and multiply, just Like God instructed us to do.

I tried to understand this statement, to process it, but all I could think of was that there is some hidden enemy behind the curtains and our only way of defeating it is through genetic engineering. I can't see the threat to our survival that only genetic engineering can cure. They might come up with one, invent it, and then throw it upon us. The options are always open.

We shall end the chapter with a 'call', made by Biologist, Lee Silver, from Princeton University: "Human beings, Now have the power not only to control but to create new genes for themselves. Why not seize the power?"

It looks like POWER is the main word defining our existence nowadays. We have forgotten completely about humbleness, ethics, and, essentially, our place in the world. The adepts of Scientism are desperately trying to drag us into their paradigm, because they feel weak on their own. With power comes control and all the horrors that follow.

The truth of the Bible is still solid, and they are deceived enough to believe that they could one day match the power of God, because that's what they want. They are empty on the inside, they are alone, and have no idea that all of this happens because they have rejected God from their lives. Their relentless struggle to replace God with something else will never bring about anything positive, only sorrow and destruction.

Chapter 12: Scientism and Sin

My little children, these things write I unto you, that ye sin not. And if any man sin, we have an advocate with the Father, Jesus Christ the righteous. 1 John 2:1

The Bible tells us about man's original sin and how the serpent (Satan) deceived Adam and Eve to eat from the forbidden tree. What followed was man's banishment from the garden of Eden and all the suffering and tribulations were a direct result of man's relation with sin.

This lesson teaches us how our actions and decisions will always have consequences and that we should always be aware that God is all knowing and that He takes notice of our wrongdoings. Jesus is the one who gave us this amazing opportunity, through his sacrifice on the cross, two thousand years ago. He chose to give up His life, so we humans can have a second chance. Jesus is the most important character, both in the old and new testament, a true Messiah, the son of God, who took the form of flesh, so that he could live among his people and show them God's glory.

The Bible depicts man's sinful nature in a way no other religion or cosmology does. It is an eye-opening statement, designed to make us understand our purpose and the purpose of our existence. Indeed, the idea of sin and responsibility put a great weight on our shoulders, but as an individual and society, because it would presume we needed to act and live our lives in a certain way, guided by the moral principle that is not always so easy to live by.

It's more and more obvious these days how certain people chose a different path, where God and the idea of sin have long been cast aside. It looks like it is easier to live your life thinking you have nothing to account for, regardless of what you do or how you hurt others.

Jesus instructed us to be kind to each other, to love our neighbors more than we would love ourselves, and even to turn the other cheek, but what we are witnessing today is far from what God wanted from us. People turned evil, hurt each other with no remorse, and looked away from their ancestral responsibility.

The new doctrine of Scientism pushed us into a grey area of exclusive materialism, where nothing else matters but to get ahead of everyone else, regardless of the means. Darwin's survival of the fittest at its finest.

Satan has worked through Scientism for centuries to deceive the masses, lately disguised in facts and proven truths. He's constantly struggling to convince us that God has nothing to do with anything and that he's just the invention of a sick human mind. He tricked us once in the garden of Eden, and he is the cause of all mankind's suffering and now he wants us to forgive, forget, and embrace him as an angel of light.

His purpose is to blind the eyes of the created to the true Creator, and for that reason, he instigates false beliefs, false truths that are supposed to make a man doubt his own existence and the existence of God at the same time.

Medical commercials to all kinds of 'extraordinary' news about new discoveries are everywhere. Now we have 9 planets, now we have 8, now we have 10… Now we have none, because people don't know what to believe anymore. We are being sold lies and false promises every day. The best way to lose weight without working out, the best way to make money without moving a finger, and so on.

For some reason, we have eliminated the struggle from our life… or at least we are trying to make it look like that.

What is this world, where nothing is really what it seems to be, and where the liars and cheaters are praised as saints, while the virtuous men are cast aside and mocked? Being a good man these days, with the fear of God, is a defect in the world we live in today, and you'll get stones thrown at you if you're trying to tell the truth for what it is.

Truth hurts most of the time, and not because the truth is harmful. On the contrary, the truth will set you free. The problem with people today is that they started enjoying living a lie and they don't want to hear about any truths. They love their lie. Satan has worked relentlessly to twist the minds of men and women, gave them this pretty lie, where nothing is forbidden, where there's no sin, no judgment day, just here and now.

With this philosophy in mind, and Scientism pushing everyone from behind, away from the Bible and the Word of God, people began to question the fabric of life.

I am sure they asked themselves, "What if there is no sin? Then we can do whatever we like and suffer no consequences!"

It all started with just one evil thought, a malevolent idea that was bound to turn the world upside down and crush the old religions and beliefs. The scientists were going to be the gods from then on and they agreed that everything was possible and permitted if you could get away with it, here on this earth.

And it's ludicrous, because God gave us this amazing chance through Jesus. Even the most sinful man in this world can rise to heavens, if he decided to repent and accept the free gift that God gives. It is a most generous offer that Scientism and its followers chose to reject, and I simply can't understand why someone in their right minds would choose to do so.

The single logical conclusion I could come up with was that they are most certainly brainwashed by Satan into believing that God means nothing and that He is the rightful ruler of the Earth. But God didn't mean to create the devil. A most beautiful arc angel called Lucifer, brighter than any sun, but with a vanity larger than God's ability to forgive.

This arc angel decided to rebel and question God's authority. His shining, angelic aura was turned into this hideous blackness that the eye rejects, and Lucifer became Satan. His envy of God was reckless and empty of meaning. His dream of grandeur ended abruptly and catastrophically.

What was once angelic joy turned into hatefulness and bitterness, a hate that will last for eternity. When Satan saw he could not get back at God directly, he swore he would attempt to corrupt God's beloved creation.

Now, we see how, little by little, we are infused with the same feeling of grandeur, and we have the same dreams of becoming more powerful than God. Unfortunately for us, we might share the same wretched fate as Satan, even if we are not aware of it just yet. Our vanity is growing by the minute, fueled by little discoveries that seem like they're at the end of the game, but we are far from there.

The truth is that we are weak. We let ourselves be fooled by Satan's wickedness, as he deceives us towards making the same mistake he did. His jealousy is endless and the lies he's selling us are as well.

Scientism is taking us away from our true meaning. Instead of exploring our souls, our consciousness, and our endless possibilities on this earth, we're being led to the dream of distant galaxies and planets, things we have no certainty exist at all.

As I write these lines, I struggle to control my anger. We have it all right here, right now, and yet, we yearn for something else. We keep chasing ghosts, while the right thing is right here under our noses. Why aren't we taking this opportunity to better ourselves, to create something real, and to make God proud of his creation? Instead, we're destroying everything, changing everything, changing people's minds and hearts, and to get what in the end? Some material gains?

I realize the depth of our sin right now, and we are getting deeper into it by the minute. There are those among us who simply refuse to see reality. They refuse to acknowledge the wonders of creation and instead of becoming more honest with themselves, they keep searching for things to improve.

It's clear to me that they're trying to show through their words and actions how God was wrong about it all and how they're going to set things right, because they can. Quite simple, isn't it?

History has shown us how hard the fall is, the higher you're trying to get, especially when your foundation is made up of smoke and feathers. That is the case with Scientism, which is trying to pose as actual science, while, in fact, it wants to become the new world religion.

It's clear as daylight, as these promoters of this new current, did not learn just yet that God is not replaceable. Jesus is the true Lord and Savior of humanity, and when the day comes, everyone will witness his might and they will feel sorry and ashamed for what they did and what they preached.

Jesus proclaimed the victory over sin with his sacrifice. He did it so that everyone could break free from the ancestral chains, and he gave us all a new chance at redemption in God's eyes. I guess this freedom was misunderstood, twisted, and transformed into something that looks nothing like the original.

Richard Dawkins said that God is a tyrant, but he is wrong! God is a forgiver and a loving creator, who will always keep His children in His arms. If all these scientists were right about the 'tyranny' part, then you would be struck by a lightning bolt at your first sin, but it does not work like that. We are all born into this life to live, to experience, and to learn the necessary lessons, before we return to God.

An open heart and a sincere prayer will always make the path to God and he will always listen to you, regardless of what other people will tell you! Jesus is the true mediator between God and man.

It's painful to see how people do not understand that Jesus sacrificed himself for us, so we can be free, and now we're heading into the trap of Scientism. A brand-new set of chains await us in the name of science, and they are ready to keep us bound forever and ever.

We emerged from an ancestral sin, which emerged from man's disobedience towards God, and now, Scientism is about to plunge us into an even greater sin. Now, God is about to exit the picture altogether, and then, we are going to be left with nothing. We will lose our identity entirely, and we're going to be stranded, just like the lost sheep in the Bible, but I don't think God will come looking for us this time.

If getting lost is something, doing it on purpose is a completely different thing. God cannot win over our hearts by force, because that's not His way. Instead, we need to acknowledge His role in our life, and we need to make room for him, without the influence of any external factors.

And now, when we're about to have that awakening moment and see the truth, there are those who claim that The Bible is nothing but a tool for controlling people, and yet they never opened it to read God's word. They dare to speak blasphemously, because they are trying to hide their actions and their purposes. Scientism is trying to pull the veil over people's eyes, but they cannot do it unless people have lost all hope and all direction. For that reason, they blame the Bible for having a hidden agenda, when, instead, they're the ones perpetrating that hideous agenda.

That's just like in the case where the wolf blames the shepherd for stealing the sheep, while the poor sheep is in his stomach already.

Those people, who are trying to control humanity right now, are fooling themselves into thinking this can be achievable. In their effort, they are creating false idolatry and trying to turn immorality into the norm, so that every person in this world would fall into sin eventually.

We can observe here how Scientism is trying to transform individuality into an amorphous mass. If we are all sinful, then sin does not exist anymore or maybe it is turned into something acceptable. After all, morality and normality are driven by the numbers. If a majority decides something to be acceptable, then they consider God has nothing to say anymore, but they are wrong. God's word can't be transformed or interpreted according to the ways of man.

With all these thoughts in mind, I have to say that the danger is still there for all of us, because we're still able to fall into their trap. Nonetheless, I hope there are those of you who are reading my words right now and acknowledging the truth about my thoughts. You must not wait anymore, you must not linger waiting for something to happen for you to understand that the truth is only found in one and we must all start looking for the one who holds the key, the only God, our true creator. Jesus.

For by him were all things created, that are in heaven, and that are in earth, visible and invisible, whether they be thrones, or dominions, or principalities, or powers: all things were created by him, and for him: Colossians 1:16

It looks to me like we have lost our connection to God lately, with all this miserable propaganda and deceiving lies. Just think about it. When was the last time you talked to God? And by this, I mean, real talk, where you closed your mind to the world and focused only on your connection with God.

I know we live in a world where everything happens on fast-forward and we feel like we don't have enough to do anymore, but this is just a false impression, created by those who want to keep our mind occupied 24/7. We all have bills to pay, mortgages to take care of, and stressful jobs that eat our energy and life, but we need to take a moment and put everything on hold, because nothing in this world is more important than God.

This is indeed a clever tactic, I must admit. Once you manage to fill up a person's head with worldly, materialistic issues and keep him stressed and confused at all times, it will be hard for anyone to think of anything else, as long as they don't know if they're going to have food on the table the next day, or if they're going to live in the same house the next month.

The sin is with them, but it's with us at the same time. With all the hardships ahead of us, we need to learn and clear our mind of all interferences. Only when we have managed to remove all the confusion and dark thoughts will we be able to really connect with God, because we need to think of Him and of Him only!

Just try, one day, to close yourself alone inside a room. Forget about your daily chores and let your mind run free. Then, try and talk to God, from the depth of your heart, and you will see how quickly things change. Your heart will soon start beating differently and a peace will engulf your soul! This is the power of God, and only He can provide this peace and serenity for us.

In a world filled with danger and 'terrorism', God wants us to live peacefully and happily. After all, we were not born into this world to make money or to turn things upside down, but to be happy and live our lives fully, regardless of what that meant for each of us.

It saddens me that we were brought to a point (the whole world, actually) where we aim at the same goals, even from an early age (big house, big car, fat bank account). Are these things the sources of our happiness? I don't think so! I have seen kids in school already indoctrinated with this false religion. When asked what they wanted to do when they grew up, so many of them simply replied: Make money!

Jesus is the way, the truth, and the life, and yet we started bowing to fake sciences and paper dollars. Is this what we actually want for humanity? Being eager to sacrifice everything and anything for things that have no intrinsic value, things that are actually destroying our life, instead of making it better? And it looks to me that everything people do nowadays is at the expense of others, the general belief being that the others are worth less than we are, and thus, they deserve such treatment from us.

We see the sun rising and setting above our heads every day, but never wonder about the power behind it. That is exactly what Scientism wants from us, to take everything for granted, thank no one for what we are given, and to ignore the wonders surrounding us. Maybe to replace God's work with something we created, to turn our faults into virtues, and to ignore the truth, even if it's right in front of our eyes.

A blinding sin supposed to alienate us from God. And then, right when we started feeling alone and scared, they can come easily from behind our backs and point us in the 'right' direction, because it's easier to fool and confuse a man when he feels scared and abandoned.

We should not let this happen to us, people! I say to you, that now, it's the right time to cover our ears, ignore the noise they're making, and focus only on what truly matters: Our Relationship with God! Sin cannot be avoided, as we're all sinners in this world, but we can always take the path of redemption. Jesus will always wait for us for, his arms wide open, as he is our shepherd, the way, the truth, the life and the only way to the true Creator of creation.

Chapter 13: Salvation from Scientism

Neither is there salvation in any other: for there is none other name under heaven given among men, whereby we must be saved.
Acts 4:12

In front of all the lies that Scientism, the mainstream media, and all the educational systems around the world throw at us, the truth stands still. We have been created by the father of all creation, the all mighty and all loving God, who made us in His image and according to His liking, regardless of what they say or how much Scientism is trying to pull us away from our creator.

You and I, and everyone else on the face of the earth, is unique and special, born into this world to fulfill a specific purpose. The random theory of evolution might be deeply rooted in society and people's minds right now, but there will always be a path for salvation, as Jesus will always have his arms wide open, for all those who are willing to embrace the truth.

In my search for the truth, I visited Fire and Grace Church in Alabama, where Pastor Dean Odle preached a sermon about the lies of Scientism and how it tries to take people away from God through false affirmations and lies, that are being spread on every level. This has been a most revelatory journey for me and an inspiring experience, as I realized that more and more people are waking up from the slumber and realizing the deception surrounding us.

People's hearts can be transformed only by listening to the Word of God, and if the amazing scripture is understood correctly. Pastor Dean explained to people how they are being used by spiritual forces for the upcoming battle over people's souls, and most importantly, how they can counteract this, in order to save themselves and those whom they love most from the face of danger.

This is only the beginning, and, little by little, I know that we can achieve great things, as more people begin to realize the true meaning of their existence. Satan has managed to transform himself into the god of this world, where materialism and money rule over everything else, and people are born and die for these things, and not for a second do they realize that their life and every breath is a gift and miracle from God and they should treat it as such.

"And ye shall know the truth, and the truth shall make you free."
John 8:32

The truth is the ultimate weapon, the ultimate goal, that will set humanity free, because man will have nothing to fear, after he understands the nature of this world and life in general. For that reason, we are being kept in the dark right now, lied to, and presented with all sorts of lies and deceptions. Scientism will become a tool for terror, eventually, but it will only be effective if people don't know the truth.

That is why I have started this journey of revelation, because I saw the bondage people are being kept in. I saw the doubt in people's hearts and the shivering of their souls, as they don't know where to look or to whom to pray to anymore.

Lately, with the new Pope, I have seen official sources, where the Vatican would like 'YOU' to accept evolution and the Big Bang. I mean, this is preposterous! The head of the Catholic Church seems like he has been infested with the Scientism virus, and now, he is trying to convince his followers that the monkey business and the big explosion out of nothing are real things.

Well, that's a low blow, don't you think? As pastor Dean says, you cannot dance around this, because the Roman Catholic Church is the bastion of Christianity in the world and its followers' number in the billions. Their approach comes with a twist though, because they did not say that the Pope does not believe in God anymore. No, no, no, they're just saying that God is still at the core of everything, but maybe God was the one who caused the Big Bang and he was the one behind the evolution process.

You see, the Pope is trying to somehow keep the Roman Catholic Church in trend with the times and maybe gain new followers, but he is doing it by twisting God's word, which is wrong. One cannot twist or interpret the Bible as they see fit, just so they can get new followers... This is not Facebook! As the head of the Roman Catholic Church, the Pope should lead people on the right path, the path of righteousness, and not bend his own teachings, according to the general social perception. Adapting God to the existing social trends is one of the greatest sins humanity has seen thus far. Also, anything the Pope is commanding people to embrace should definitely raise red flags with those that have proper discernment.

In essence, they are trying to underline the fact that they believe the theories of Scientism, regarding what scripture says. Is it wrong, is it right for people to follow this new trend of faith? I will let you decide for yourself, after you go through some of the things I'll talk about onwards.

This new approach is another way of saying 'religion' is a 'worldview,' the whole of reality. The evolutionary worldview applies not only to the evolution of life, but even to that of the entire universe. In the realm of cosmic evolution, our naturalistic scientists depart even further from experimental science than life scientists do, manufacturing a variety of evolutionary cosmologies from esoteric mathematics and metaphysical speculation. Social theorist, Jeremy Rifkin, has commented on this remarkable game saying:

"Cosmologies are made up small snippets of physical reality that have been remodeled by society into vast cosmic deceptions."

So, this sort of ideology has infested everything and it goes everywhere, from one corner of the universe to the other, so do you get your cosmology from the Bible or do you get it from those people? A bunch of delusional maniacs, who think they are above

God, just because they had a crazy idea that's been accepted by a bunch of people?

Scientism is not science, it has never been and was never meant to be! This 21st century religion is more of an esoteric religion, meant to twist people's hearts and perceptions. You can see the evilness in their eyes, every time you mention the Bible, and how their pupils catch fire. We all know the eyes are the mirror of the soul, and this so-called Scientism's prophets have a dark soul, full of evil intentions.

Being accountable might be the scariest thing in the world, therefore, these people have cast God aside and chosen for themselves another divinity, one closer to the ancient times, where gods and goddesses expected from humanity not truth and righteousness, but bribes and material things. That's why Scientism is so embedded in the occult, and it does not even take an ancient form, but it praises the same elements (greed, materialism, self-sufficiency), but dressed in a scientific coat, masked by good intentions.

This is the main reason why adepts of Scientism do not love and accept the light, because light exposes sin and all their wrongful deeds. In the shadows, they will always look immaculate, even if, on the inside, they are dark and rotten.

They are wrong about it! Whether they know it or not, stepping into the light is the only way for us to cleanse our souls and accepting our sins is the first step of this endeavor. Like in the case of cancer, you cannot get a cure, if you don't admit you are ill in the first place. It is the same with sin. If you don't accept the fact that you are a sinner, you will never accept the savior into your life. You must be convinced that you are a sinner, that you have broken the laws of God, that you have broken the commandments that God, our Creator, gave us.

You need to feel that guilt, you need to feel that shame, and accept the fact that you are a sinner in the eyes of God. The moment you accept this reality, you will get to the point where you will be able to say: I need to find forgiveness and redemption, I need to find this Creator and beg for forgiveness in front of Him… And God will forgive you and accept you into His arms.

The good news for all true believers is that God, Jesus Christ, came to Earth in the flesh and sacrificed Himself for us, by dying on the cross, for us to find forgiveness and redemption. The gospel says it clearly, for all those who have eyes to see and ears to hear, that Jesus, the son of God, is our last and only hope. Through him we can reach the kingdom of heaven, but first, we must accept and embrace him and accept the fact that we are not without sin in the face of God.

We are not meant to go to hell, or to be separated from God, but for us to reach heaven and sit next to our Creator for eternity, we need to repent first.

Jesus died so that his blood would wash away the sins of mankind. There are people who have forgotten the meaning of his sacrifice a long time ago, but it is time for all of us to remember and understand why the Jesus came down to earth. Humanity was once soaking in sin and Jesus wiped it all out, through his death and resurrection, and it remained as a free gift, till the end of days.

You need to understand that you don't have to do this through a certain church. This sacred connection is made between you and Jesus, and you can get down on your knees anytime, anywhere and say, ", I believe! Please, show me the right way!" and God will answer you. Remember that the number one way that God speaks to you is through His Word, the Bible.

"Ask, and it shall be given you; seek, and ye shall find; knock, and it shall be opened unto you." Matthew 7:7

These few words can be categorized as the core of Jesus' teaching, while walking on the face of this earth. He will not come into your life to work wonders for you, if you don't ask him to come first. He created us and it is our decision whether we want to believe in Him or fully surrender to Him or not.

Whether it's creation, salvation, or the end of times, the only book that has it all right is the Bible, the Word of God. In the Bible, you will find everything ahead of time, and now, tell me if there is one man in this world who knows what it will happen thousands of years from now. Forget Nostradamus and all the other crooks, who pretended to know something, when in fact they did not know anything.

The Bible explains what is going to happen from day one, until the end of times. The words written on its pages are infallible, they are truth that's going to be revealed to all humanity at the end of times, and every man, woman, and child will realize how wrong they were to believe in something else.

Now, it's time for you to get a hold of the truth. Stop believing all the zeitgeist lies and all the other foolishness that comes along with them, because they have no idea what they are talking about and all they have is a bunch of assumptions that stand in midair, with no solid foundation.

I know it is not easy, as the devil has been attacking the Bible for centuries, and from all angles, but I am asking you to stay strong, because the Bible is still here, and it's proven to be true. With all the scheming and malevolent interpretation, the Bible managed to prove to people repeatedly that God and His word are Holy and eternal. Despite modern belief and the plethora of insults coming from all sides, you should not be ashamed by your belief in the Bible. If you know this to be true, you have nothing to be ashamed of. In the end, all those who think they know better and who mock those who choose to believe the world of the holy scripture will be shown how wrong they were, and they will suffer the consequences of their choice.

Heaven is our salvation and the Gospel of Jesus Christ is the path we need to walk to reach God's kingdom. Our Lord will come back to earth and he will judge us all, those who have chosen the path of true faith will be rewarded, while those, who, in their stubbornness, chose to defy God and his teachings, will suffer the consequences. The true Creator of creation is calling out to you. Will you heed His call?

The following prayer expresses the desire to transfer trust to Christ alone for eternal salvation. If its words speak of your own heart's desire, praying them can be the link that will connect you to God.

Dear God, I know that I am a sinner and there is nothing that I can do to save myself. I confess my complete helplessness to forgive my own sin or to work my way to heaven. At this moment I trust Christ alone as the One who bore my sin when He died on the cross. I believe that He did all that will ever be necessary for me to stand in your holy presence. I thank you that Christ was raised from the dead as a guarantee of my own resurrection. As best as I can, I now transfer my trust to Him. I am grateful that He has promised to receive me despite my many sins and failures. Father, I take you at your word as the true Creator of all creation. I thank you that I can face death now that you are my Savior. Thank you for the assurance that you will walk with me through the deep valley. Thank you for hearing this prayer. In Jesus' Name. Amen.

Chapter 14: Conclusions to the book

*The thing that hath been, it is that which shall be; and that which
is done is that which shall be done: and there is no new thing
under the sun. Ecclesiastes 1:9*

In conclusion, I would like to reiterate the importance of the Bible
in our life. We might be subjected to all sorts of lies and
deceptions, from the moment we open our eyes in the morning until
we set our head on the pillow in the evening, but this is no reason
for us to reject God and start believing all these false prophecies.

You have seen already, as you have read through the chapters of
my book, that, right now, we are in the middle of a war over our
hearts, and I am telling you that there is no greater danger for us. If
we abandon our faith, we are lost, because, without God, nothing
can be achieved in this world. The arrogant people might think they
hold the answers to everything, but they are wrong, and, in the end,
they will realize that science is nothing but another tool created by
God to help humanity.

Under the influence of Satan, people have turned true science
into Scientism, an evil philosophy that is struggling to become the
new world religion and replace Christianity altogether.

It is up to us, the faithful, to decide if their efforts will have any
success, because they cannot achieve anything if we don't accept it
Fortunately, we still have time to change our minds, as we are not
living under a scientist dictatorship, but the clock is ticking already,
and time is becoming limited, with every passing day.

Just think of it. Would you like to live in a world of truth, where
God is recognized as our true Creator of creation and a loving father,
a world of the free, where each individual has the right to choose
their own path in life (with no external influences/pressures) and
answer for his decisions? It's clear to me that our world is in danger,

and more and more voices are shouting that those who choose not to believe in Scientism must be punished.

Upon close analysis, Scientism is not so different from Communism. They both hold the same beliefs. As a matter of fact, I already mentioned how Scientism is the foundation of communism and we all know what happened. Millions died, and even more millions suffered in pain and hunger. If communism managed to conquer only part of the world and there were still forces that could fight it, now, Scientism wants to take over the whole world, and once we are trapped, we will have no chance to break free, and they know it.

For that reason and more, it is imperative for us to understand the extent of the danger we are being subjected to right now, as I write these lines. We need to stand together in truth and disclose their lies. We must put all those claims under the revelatory light of God and show the world their treachery. I know it is not going to be easy, but the satisfaction at the end will surpass anything else you have felt in your life.

I'm sure you have felt already what being free means. Unfortunately, there are people in this world who have lost this sense of freedom and truth. After so many years of lies and propaganda, they have fallen to Scientism, but they are not lost. Jesus is waiting for all of us to step into his kingdom. All we must do is realize and accept who our true Creator is, our Father and our salvation.

Those of you who have already understood the truth are fortunate and I can say that, together, we have a mission to bring the people around us onto the right path, and, with a common effort, we can eventually bring many back into the arms of God.

Major lies we will be subjected to:

- There is no creator and they will put forth false proof, backing their statements.

- Religion has been crippling mankind for more than two millennia and we need to get rid of it, if we ever want to advance as a species. Religion is nothing but a relic of the past and we need to get rid of it, as we are too advanced to believe in ancient fables now.

- The Bible is not the Word of God, but a mixture of false texts, written by false prophets, thus, it's fake and untrustworthy.

- Aliens are really out there, and they are far superior to us (again, we will get proof of their existence, maybe a sort of face to face meeting)

- The occult mysteries are, in fact, the truth we had been seeking for so many years. They will replace the Bible.

- Our whole life is nothing but an illusory construct (if you look carefully, we can see people like Elon Musk and other scientists who clam we live inside a simulation and that nothing is actually real. What we feel and live is only the game of a sick alien, who could not find another way to have fun).

- Media will jump on our backs more and more and refer to their past accounts, just to prove to us that they were right in the first place, when they were talking about aliens, the earth being a planet, and all the other accounts.

- The fallen angels, the ones who disobeyed God's word and have fallen in disgrace along with Satan, will come and pose as gods and our true creators. Scientism will entertain this idea and will try to convince people to embrace this new idea and cast God aside in the process. One of God's creations will fight against God and mankind at the same time, and only those of true faith will come out victorious from this battle.

- Last, but not the least, the antichrist will come to us as a savior, a messiah we needed so much, the man who will finally restore the truth to this world. But first, Scientism and those involved in the process will create all the necessary problems, thus creating the urgency for a messiah. Even now, we have all the solutions for all the problems, but we are not solving anything, or at least trying to. The plan is for us to get in deep problems and start thinking we need someone else to resolve the situation for us.

We all need to remain vigilant in an age of misinformation and deceit and to always look for the source of that information. Sometimes, we might get good-sounding, good-looking, but, nonetheless, false information, thus, we need to beware of false prophets, people who pretend to speak the true Word of God, while, in fact, they are speaking the language of Satan.

"Beloved, believe not every spirit, but try the spirits whether they are of God: because many false prophets are gone out into the world.

Hereby know ye the Spirit of God: Every spirit that confesseth that Jesus Christ is come in the flesh is of God: And every spirit that confesseth not that Jesus Christ is come in the flesh is not of God: and this is that spirit of antichrist, whereof ye have heard that it should come; and even now already is it in the world." 1 John 4:1-3

I believe I have given you enough food for thought for you to continue your research. And remember, the truth has the nasty habit of always coming to the surface eventually. No lie is elaborate enough to last forever, and I believe we are smart enough to make the distinction between the lies of Scientism and the Word of God, which is, indeed, the ultimate truth. I pray that you will come to know the true Creator of creation and His Will for your life.

About the Author

 Robbie Davidson is the founder of Celebrate Truth which has produced ground-breaking documentary films such as The Global Lie & the latest Scientism Exposed (2016) & Scientism Exposed 2 (2017) reaching millions of people across the world. His YouTube Channel 'Celebrate Truth' has over 100,000 subscribers.

He is also the organizer of the Flat Earth International Conference (FEIC). With a passion for media & film making his desire is to help expose the world's lies while pointing people to the way, the truth and the life (John 14:6). He was not always a man of faith. Much of his early education and worldview was held by the "so called truth" of what Scientism had taught him.

After becoming a Christian at the age of 21 he attended Northwest Baptist College & Trinity Western University and has been involved in various faith-based media organizations throughout his career. Robbie lives in Edmonton, Alberta. Canada and is married to Rachel and has two daughters, Kiara and Sophia and one son Robbie Jr.

Contact Information

Robbie Davidson
7551-152 B Ave. NW
Edmonton, Alberta
T5C 3M6 Canada
1-780-993-9004
robbied@gmail.com
CelebrateTruth.org

YOU WON'T BELIEVE WHAT YOU SEE AND HEAR!

SCIENTISM EXPOSED

Hiding the True Creator of Creation

Scientism Exposed 1 & 2 Available on DVD and Digital Download.

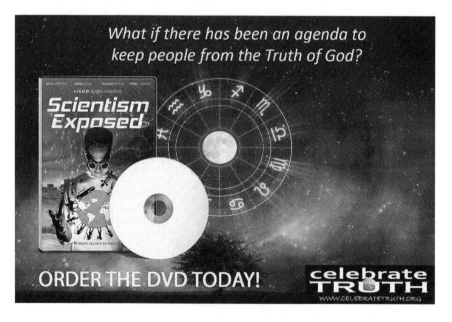

For more information go to CelebrateTruth.org

30279055R00119

Printed in Poland
by Amazon Fulfillment
Poland Sp. z o.o., Wrocław